19

A THREEFOLD CORD

A THREEFOLD CORD

by

MAUDE ROYDEN
(MRS. HUDSON SHAW)

NEW YORK
THE MACMILLAN COMPANY
1948

First Printing

"A threefold cord is not quickly broken."
(Eccles. 4. 12.)

ILLUSTRATIONS

In the text

FOREWORD

THIS BOOK is written by my husband's wish. Over and over again during his lifetime he said how he wished there might be some written record of our story. We planned to write it together, but our lives were very full and it was never even begun. Now that I am alone and the other two of our threefold love have left me, I take joy in attempting what he so much wished might be done: partly for his sake because he wished it, partly for mine because it is, even in solitude, a joy to recall our great happiness; and partly also for the sake of his friends and mine, whose love and confidence in us deserves—and encourages me to offer—this inadequate story of what we were to one another. "We" means we three always: Hudson Shaw, Effie Shaw, and myself.

MAUDE ROYDEN SHAW.

CHAPTER I

H UDSON SHAW and I met for the first time in Oxford in 1901. We loved each other at sight.

We did not realize this at first. He was in Oxford for the University Extension Summer School at which he was a great and beloved personality, lecturing brilliantly and wanted everywhere by everyone. I had only gone down from Lady Margaret Hall a year or two before, and I attended partly as a student, but chiefly because a friend of mine was Assistant Secretary to the Delegacy; and anyhow I always wanted an excuse to be in Oxford.

Hudson was lecturing on Ruskin, whom he idolized. I detested Ruskin for his conceited attitude towards women, and had never recovered from an early disgust created by *Sesame and Lilies*. But Hudson's lectures were magnificent and, though not permanently converted to his view of Ruskin, I was carried away by the lecturer.

I was at that time in much perplexity about my religion. The Roman Catholic Church attracted me and I could not find rest for my soul. Hudson was a parson, and as he was willing to talk the matter over with me I went to see him. I arrived at his lodgings in Merton Street a little early: he was out. I sat, feeling nervous, and looked out of the window on to that enchanting street. Is it enchanting still? Yes, I think so. I never drive through Oxford without going there to sit and remember.

Very soon Hudson came in. I heard his footsteps coming up the stairs. I hear them still. Is it Maeterlinck who says one should always listen to approaching footsteps with awe and expectation for one knows not who is coming into one's life?

We talked of many things and parted with regret. But

before leaving Oxford we had one more meeting, this time on the river. We spent a long afternoon together and, as we came back to the landing-place at Magdalen Bridge, I looked up at the great tower. When I brought my eyes back into the boat I saw that Hudson was watching me. "It's that sort of thing that knocks you over, isn't it?" he said.

Many years after, when I was asked to broadcast in a series "Why I believe in God", and began "I believe in God because of Beauty", I remembered that day. Some of my hearers were shocked and wrote to tell me so. However, it remains true. It *is* because of Beauty that, at the worst, I have never disbelieved in God, and it has been the care for beauty in the Roman Catholic Church that has sometimes made me homesick for it.

The Summer School ended. We all left Oxford and I hardly expected that I should see Hudson again. I wrote, however, to thank him for his kindness to me and he replied:—

"Truly, I think it is my gratitude that is due to you. It was a real joy to talk to you and listen to you. I have lived so long now with the jog-trot and the ordinary, the cool, practical folk, that it was absolutely refreshing to meet someone burnt up with enthusiasm and not ashamed of it. You have done me good. . . . I hope you will let the Eternal Problem rest a while. I can see you are tired of never-ending questionings. After all, God will be with you, whether you remain Anglican or must find rest with Rome, and 'he that *willeth* to do His will shall know of the doctrine'. . . . Work is not the sovereign remedy that Carlyle thought, but it settles many problems."

This was to be true for us in ways we did not dream of then.

I think it was Hudson's patience with me that won in the end. I hardly remember now the lines on which we argued out the theological case, but I remember well his insistence

on my not deciding in a hurry, and on the absolute importance of not accepting anything which involved compromise
with my conscience. The appeal which Rome makes to
many, and not least to me, is partly one of temperament and,
since the concerns of the soul are deeper and higher than
reason, it is hard not to let temperament prevail over reason.
This Hudson would never let me do. I must not, he said,
through weariness of spirit or perplexity of mind, "swallow"
what I did not with heart and soul accept as true. I feel sure
that the wisest Roman Catholics would give the same advice
and insist on the same endurance and if, in the end, they
must feel that I decided wrongly, they would hold this a
better end than to accept and then repent and repudiate
acceptance. What I want here to emphasize is the intellectual honesty and long-suffering endurance of an adviser
who could say so earnestly—"If in the end you feel you must
go, God be with you." Nor was this patience for me only.
It was characteristic of Hudson's attitude towards all seekers,
and a passage I found in a letter to him years afterwards expresses it. "Never shall I forget or cease to be grateful for
your unspeakable kindness to me in my callow questing
youth." How many students knew the same "unspeakable
personal kindness" to them in their callow questing youth!

At first, and for a long time afterwards, we were unaware
of any personal problem. Looking back, I find it easy to see
why. I was seventeen years younger than Hudson and he
was a man already widely known, both in this country and
America; a brilliant lecturer and much more than that—a
leader of men, with life dedicated to a cause which to the
end of his life never ceased to hold him—the education of
the democracy. I was a mere schoolgirl in my own eyes,
compared with him. I set him on a pedestal and never
thought of him as an equal. Perhaps I was already old
enough to laugh at myself a little—I was twenty-four, but
the young didn't grow up so quickly in those days, and
though I knew I was being a little schoolgirlish about it, this

only made it easier for me to remain unconscious of my real feeling for Hudson. I knew I had found in him a magnetic and powerful personality and I was delighted that his interest in my difficulties did not end with our first interview: beyond that I did not look.

And he? He found in me a response to the things he most cared for in life—religion and the great cause. He, too, felt the difference in our ages, and it is significant that while our friendship increased both he and Effie (Mrs. Shaw) for many years always called me "Child" and he even, in a letter I still have, worked out a nice little sum:—

$$"44 - 26 = 18."$$

"Therefore you might have been, therefore by my logic you are my Child!"

Actually, I always held that there was only seventeen years between us, his birthday being in August and mine in November. So he would have been a very juvenile parent.

Effie, and I also, always called Hudson "the Man", as if there was only one!

It was very natural. We were both the product of our time and circumstances. Both had been brought up in the Church of England. Hudson was a parson and I absorbed at the time in purely religious problems. The very idea of his loving anyone but his wife, or I loving a married man, could not enter our heads. If it had, we should, I am certain, have parted not to meet again. We had not enough knowledge of life or of the human heart to guess of what it is capable in love nor how many ways there are of loving.

We agreed, therefore, to meet again and meanwhile to continue our discussions by correspondence. I went to work in a Settlement in Liverpool (my home being in the north of Cheshire), and Hudson returned to his tiny parish in Rutland and his large public in University Extension work.

After I had been at the Settlement for two years I succumbed to overwork. Naturally, I turned to Hudson for counsel. My breakdown was due to the fact that my lameness had been diagnosed, by a number of eminent orthopædists, as hysteria and, X-rays not being then in common use, I was told I could walk quite well if I chose. I couldn't, but naturally I tried, being a little troubled by the fear that I could "if I chose", and that I had been making a fuss about nothing.

I speak of the *fear* I had because I have always thought it was better to have dislocated hips than a dislocated mind. So, in one way, it was a relief that the X-ray photographs revealed that it was my hips that were dislocated even though, in those days, it was too late for any surgical treatment to be of any use. Sir Robert Jones' only consolation was that none of the many surgeons I had seen had "done me any harm"—a fact on which my mother and I warmly congratulated each other as we departed. Still, it is a pest to be lame, and one result of the certainty that I was lame and would be so always has its importance in this story. It made me believe that I should never marry.

I have been told that my lameness only made those who loved me love me more, and I know now that that can be true. Men can be very chivalrous. One man even assured me with admirable gravity that, if I ever had a daughter and wanted her to marry, I had nothing to do but ill-treat her at home and men would hurry to the rescue of the poor little thing! I have an adopted daughter, but have never been able to adopt this no doubt excellent expedient, partly because I could not be perfectly convinced of its invariable success and partly because she married too early for me to make the experiment. But that a lover can love the beloved all the more for pity I do know. How often has Hudson said to me—"I want you to be cured of your lameness—I would give anything for you to be cured—but, for myself, I should miss it." I don't think anything more sweet and consoling to the heart than this can ever be said by one human being to another. Only those who suffer from some such physical defect as mine can understand how sweet. It is our secret and our balm. Nevertheless, I did not believe it for a long time. *I* knew what a nuisance lameness was and I could not believe that, whatever a man might feel about it at first, he would not feel it to be a nuisance in the end. And so I remained sure that I should not marry and that my life must be lived some other way.

I write this here because it serves to show why, when Hudson asked me to go and help him as a sort of unpaid curate in his little country parish, I could and did joyfully accept the suggestion without a shadow of hesitation or fear of my own feelings—or his. My attempt to walk "as much and as well as anybody" had ended in weariness so great that a change had to be made. Hudson offered me, instead of work in a great city, a retreat in the country, where rectory, church, and school stood close together, with a population of less than three hundred clustered round them. If I needed anything more I had a bicycle. Mrs. Shaw, I understood, was an invalid, Hudson much away Extension lecturing, and the vicar of the parish next door within call for any emergency.

My mother, already resigned to the eccentric behaviour of her youngest daughter, accompanied me on a visit to South Luffenham.

I suffered the agonies of all who introduce an admired and beloved friend to a doubting parent with less than no confidence in the judgment of her progeny. My fears were realized; Hudson and my mother shouted to each other across a wide, wide gulf. In vain did I offer topic after topic suitable for polite conversation. Each was dropped with a heavy thud. And Effie—Mrs. Shaw—did nothing to help.

It was my first meeting with her. Every memory of it is engraved on my heart.

Hudson had met us—my mother and me—at the station and brought us up to the rectory. Effie stood awaiting us in the drawing-room.

Dear, strange, enchanting Effie! How shall I convey to strangers the kind of spirit she was whose spirit was so unlike any of us? I think Shelley might have described her, for she, if like anyone, was like him. If not a poet she was a musician, an artist, and a wit. She had an unearthly grace and charm and other-worldliness. But I heap words on words and none find her.

For with all her gifts, there was a strange spell on her—a shyness almost frantic sometimes, a fear of life which lay on her like frost upon a flower.

That night she stood looking at us and I did not guess at the shyness that held her. I fell in love with her, too, at first sight. This was the real beginning of the love that changed all our three lives. If she had not loved me and I her, what happened afterwards would have been impossible.

CHAPTER II

IN SPITE of their inability to understand each other, my mother and Hudson agreed that there was no reason why I should not be his curate for a time, and in the autumn of 1905 I went to South Luffenham "on approval". I did all the usual things that parish workers do: visited the needy, coached some girls who wanted to be teachers, took evening classes for those who had left school but still didn't know everything, taught in the Sunday School—a task for which I was quite curiously incompetent—and fetched in the near-by parson to do all the things a woman wasn't allowed to do. Hudson was at home a day or two in the week and, of course, always on Sundays, when I "sat under him", listening with intense interest to his sermons and with exasperation to his reading of the lessons. I didn't dream of preaching sermons, but how I longed to read lessons! After all, I thought, why not?

Well, it was *not* in those days. On one occasion, when Hudson had a week's mission, preached by a friend, in South Luffenham, he asked (or ordered?) me to speak at the last service. For this purpose the congregation had to be marshalled in procession and marched off to the schoolroom where it sat in acute discomfort, crowded, asphyxiated, and in children's desk-seats, to hear me explain "Why I am a Christian". I was so frightened that I don't remember anything but feeling quite sick, and can only repeat the remark of a friend of mine who, being asked how she had got on with her first speech, answered with joy "I heard every word I said."

For the first three months we were all "on approval", I to them and they to me—but for me there was never any doubt. I have some of the letters I wrote home at this time, full of almost hysterical adoration for these two marvellous beings. In years I was far from a schoolgirl, but I was a slow grower and, as I loved Hudson and Effie with the same unreasoning devotion, I saw no difference betwen the two. I loved them both and thought them the most wonderful people in the world. They loved me and Hudson wrote to a friend of mine that I had "changed his wife's life for her".

When I was going home for Christmas at the end of the three months' "approval", Hudson asked me if I was coming back, and I, delighted to be wanted, said I would "if he wanted me". "Want you?" he cried with a voice of sudden passion that shook me, "*Want* you? If you could know the chill, the horror, that falls on me when I think you won't come!"

I remember the tone of his voice now, and still it shakes me. It is forty-three years ago and it has been so with us always—a chill and a horror if the other "does not come".

At that time I was startled and even bewildered. Then I put it out of my mind or only delighted in the knowledge that my prophet-hero wanted me. I was undaunted by the fact that he was himself going away almost immediately for a long lecture tour in America. I was to take care of Effie during his absence and carry on the work entrusted to me.

For it was understood that Effie was an invalid and must not be expected to work. That was really why I was needed: I understood that. What I did not understand was Effie herself. I adored her, but I hardly knew her. I had no idea of the almost frenzied shyness that often made her speechless. I was perplexed and, no doubt, stupid. She could not understand why I babbled like a brook when Hudson was there and fell into unaccountable silences when he was not. The idea that conversation cannot be a monologue was one she never got hold of. It was, she held, easy for me to talk and difficult for her. Why then did I not talk, whether Hudson was there or not? It could only be that I thought her not

worth talking to! While I sweated and toiled to find subjects of conversation with one whom I loved to desperation,
but hardly knew at all, she sat in an island of silence and
dropped every ball I sent across. The result was much mis-
understanding and even tears. I re-read now letters that I
wrote to her when I happened to be away for a night or two,
and which she kept, and I am filled with amusement and
amazement. They are hysterical in their devotion and
despair. I loved her and could not bear to fail her while
Hudson was away. I loved him and felt he had entrusted to
me her happiness and well-being, and I was failing him too.

I am sure Effie never knew what I suffered, and only a
very immature young woman could have suffered in just
that way. I am amazed at myself. But those months set a
mark on me that I have never lost, and I was older by much
more than four months when Hudson came back from
America.

I didn't know that my adored Effie, with all her strange
and lovely charm, was mentally unstable and possessed by
an overwhelming fear of life. I didn't know that Hudson
was, to her, strength and security and that, without him, no
one, however loved, could save her from that strange terror
of which she once said to me that "if she only knew what she
was afraid of she wouldn't be afraid".

Effie *never* felt safe when Hudson was not there.

He came back and we rejoiced. Conversation flowed.
Effie listened and was most content to listen. She used to
laugh at us, or perhaps it would be more true to say that she
and I together laughed at Hudson and she and he together
laughed at me.

It is a commonplace to say that people who love each
other find themselves laughing at the same things, but it is
not always true. Hudson and I rarely laughed at the same
things: Effie and I always did. Hudson was transported with
glee at things that left us cold. He used to say we had no
sense of humour, but he only meant that we hadn't his sense

of humour. It never strikes me as really funny when someone sits on his hat or plays a practical joke which almost
always hurts someone else's feelings. I loathe practical jokes.
So did Effie. Hudson adored them, and it was only after
several painful explosions on my part that he realized my sad
lack of humour and stopped playing them on me. He turned
the garden hose on me in my best pale grey *crêpe de Chine*
frock, and that was the end of that.

Effie and I thought him funny in quite a different way and
we laughed ourselves to exhaustion at him, but he only
regarded us with indulgent pity and said, "Silly women!"

Our talk was not all theological. Hudson had a historian's
mind and history was his subject as a University Extension
lecturer. He would gaze in rapture at a plough and urge us
all to realize that ploughs and plough-shares "just that shape"
had been used by men for centuries. The thought of it
almost (so Effie and I used to say) moved him to tears, but
he, I must add, continually moved us to mirth. After a visit
to Palestine, Hudson, having removed a pair of muddy and
not well-tree'd shoes, held them up and exclaimed with
immense solemnity: "These boots have trodden the streets
of Jericho."

History and theology here met for our edification. We
were edified, though we laughed.

We discussed politics unendingly. Effie was a Conservative, Hudson a Liberal, and I a mug-wump on my way from
a Conservative beginning to a Socialist end. (I never joined
any party, however, till I had the vote.) I had been brought
up to think of the royal family with great esteem and of
Queen Victoria with reverence. Hudson derided these views
and thought them comic, but he was almost as odd a mixture
as I was, for he stoutly upheld the State Church of England
and attacked the Education Bill of 1906 with vehemence.
On the question of the Establishment I remember a debate in
the schoolroom at South Luffenham—Hudson speaking for,
a railway porter against, and I in the chair. The village was

divided between delight and horror at the spectacle of the rector being opposed by one of his own flock and cheered the porter loudly; but when it came to the vote they were all for the rector.

A debate on a much larger scale was arranged between Hudson and a neighbouring Free Church minister when the Education Act was before the country. The local farmers were all on Hudson's side and would stop in the road to beg him not to lose his temper as he would certainly win his case if he kept it. He was delighted with this advice, though it was really unnecessary, for I never knew him lose his temper in debate, public or private. He and I discussed the Bill from morning till night for, though we both opposed it, we did so for completely different reasons. I wanted Hudson to see how illogical he was, while he was sure I did see how illogical I was, though, out of perversity, I would not admit it.

We discussed another burning question which was later to take me into another sphere of work—Women's Suffrage. I was already a believer in it, but not a well-instructed one.

"Women can't vote because they can't be soldiers and defend the matters they vote for," said Hudson.

I was baffled.

"Isn't that so?" he insisted.

"Yes," I said.

He was staggered, never having believed that one could be convinced of error by argument. Then he set to work to find the answer to his own objection in the hope that I would then argue back. I don't think he ever really wanted to convince me, for in that case he would have had no one to argue with. Effie never entered the fray, and his sister, who occasionally came to stay, had been brought up to regard him with a superstitious reverence which forbade discussion.

One day he invited us to hear him read his latest lecture. It was on some matter of Roman history, and as it wound along I saw with horror what the end would be. It came as I feared—"butchered to make a Roman holiday"! I uttered a cry of pain—"Oh, Man, *must* we have that?" Hudson burst out laughing, but Miss Shaw was appalled. Never had she heard Hudson criticized before. She begged him to disregard the impertinence. He did. The butchery remained.

It was a marvel that Hudson was as humble-minded as, essentially, he was, for his women relations were Victorian in their attitude to the male. Effie's mother—Hudson's aunt, for he and Effie were first cousins—was a witty and most lovable old lady with a strong mind and strong opinions of her own; but she, too, was known to have said, when Effie and I were talking some nonsense—"Hush! Hudson is going to speak!" After this, whenever Hudson opened his mouth, Effie and I were liable to raise our hands in admonition and say to each other—"Hush! Hudson is going to speak!" Effie indeed never adopted the reverential attitude of sister and aunt. She was incapable of it. Perhaps that saved Hudson—or would have done if he had needed saving, but his real humility was utterly untainted by conceit. He was always deeply aware of his insufficient education and lack of scholarship, and asked all the best theologians to his schools and churches to teach his flock the things he felt himself inadequately equipped to teach. I was, however, delighted when once, after listening respectfully to a theologian of repute instructing his class, Hudson could not refrain from murmuring in my ear—"I believe I know a lot more about it than he does!"

I don't think anyone who lived with Hudson could help laughing at him. He was often so enchantingly absurd! He was always convinced that everyone wanted what he wanted and generally we did. When we didn't it did not make the slightest difference: he did it all the same. No one was more earnest in asking advice and none disregarded it more completely. Soon after my arrival at South Luffenham he took it into his head that the church needed a new organ. As was always the case with him when a new interest seized him, nothing else was spoken of or thought about for months. It was a wonder that so small an object could arouse such ardour. So small was it that we could not decide whether it should have four stops or six. Round this difficult point discussion raged. We had it for breakfast, for lunch, tea, and dinner. At last while interest and argument were still at their height, Hudson remarked casually that we needn't worry ourselves as he had already given the order for six.

Effie was delighted at my fury. He always behaved like that, she said—and he always did. He was quite sure we should find that he was right. If we didn't—but then he didn't notice that, and we were obliged to give up noticing it too.

He always had the most admirable reasons for acting as he did. I remember one occasion when a really terrible lapse had occurred in connection with some parish affair. It was in no sense Hudson's fault, and when a very high dignitary of the Church—in fact, the Archbishop of Canterbury*—wrote a really charming letter asking for an explanation, Hudson was for days and even weeks poised on the brink of a letter in reply. In spite of entreaties, he remained poised. I offered secretarial help, I stressed the urgency of the occasion and the extraordinary kindness of the Archbishop, but all was vain. While agreeing that the letter must be written and des-patched at once, Hudson pointed out in return that (a) it would be discourteous to send a typed letter, (b) it must be very carefully considered, (c) it was now too late to write at all. Years afterwards when I referred gloomily to this abominable affair, Hudson solemnly assured me that his *real* reason for not writing was that he hated to add to the Archbishop's over-laden mail bag.

As a matter of fact, Hudson was almost physically in-capable of writing letters at all. As usual he thought that this was a perfectly good explanation of his horrid conduct. Sir Charles Mallet told me he had once met him rushing along a

* Dr. Cosmo Gordon Lang.

London street and, stopping him almost by violence, had said—

"I wrote to you months ago. Why have you never answered my letter?"

"I don't write letters," said Hudson.

"I know you don't," said Sir Charles, "but why don't you?"

Hudson thought this an extraordinarily silly question.

For my part (though he did write to me) I have often marvelled at the number of his friends and their abiding affection for him in the face of his long silences. They loved him all the same and, in the end, I believe, admitted that to ask him why he didn't write to them was extraordinarily silly.

Life with him was always interesting, often infuriating, sometimes, in fits of depression, almost tragic; but never dull.

With this magnetic, explosive personality, I lived and worked in a little isolated country parish for three years.

CHAPTER III

OUR LOVE for each other grew. We went on thinking of it as fatherly on his side and hero-worship on mine. Then suddenly, as a crystal is formed by a shake of the glass, our awareness crystallized.

The shake was given by a friend who, for a wonder, was actually staying at the rectory for a long visit. She was older than I and far more a woman of the world. She saw what was happening to us and, very kindly, gave me a word of advice. I—like an idiot—was amazed and enraged. Her friendly warning seemed to me an attempt to poison an innocent and happy relationship which was my dearest possession. Like the bull in a china-shop which all my life I have too closely resembled, I rushed straight to Hudson and poured out my indignation and disgust. "She thinks I'm in love with you," I roared. And he roared too, for Hudson also a little resembled the china-shop bull. We mingled our indignation and our plaints. I blush now to think of our injustice to our mutual friend. We didn't even trouble to assure each other that we were not in love: the idea still seemed preposterous. We didn't think of it. It could not be. That was enough.

It was not enough. Effie knew what was happening. She saw that, unconsciously, we were already living under a great strain. I, at least, had reached a point at which the smallest disagreement, the slightest difference, between Hudson and myself was unbearable. I became irritable and quarrelsome, never with her but often with him.

No doubt the nature of my work made life difficult for me. Hudson loved his village and his pastoral work, but it could never have satisfied him. His energy, his need for the society of his intellectual equals and the give and take of the world, demanded exactly such an outlet as University Extension lecturing gave him. I had no such relief. My life was confined to a tiny village—and Hudson and Effie. Much as I loved them, I strained at the leash.

Of this at least I was conscious, and Hudson was conscious too. He determined that I should live as he did, between the little world of home and village life, and the world outside. He pushed the Oxford University Extension Delegacy into giving me a trial, and he pushed University Extension centres into inviting me to lecture.

It is not my intention here to tell the story of my life outside our love. Here, then, I leave it aside except to record the fact that it was Hudson Shaw who first made me think I could be a speaker: he who by sheer force of determination opened the world of lecturing to me: he who helped me, advised me, taught me, believed in me, made others believe in me. In after years, when he took delight in any success I won, I used to tell him he had created me. He scoffed. I know it is true. Without him—but I can't conceive my life without him.

Or without Effie. If Hudson and I knew our minds, she knew our hearts. Whether she too received a friendly warning from our friend I do not know, but I think it may have been so. Her reaction to it was as surprising as mine. She believed that I could never have all I needed as long as Hudson gave to me, and I to him, no more than affection, no more than friendship. She was aware that we sometimes, in spite of friendship, got on each other's nerves. Hudson, at least, got on mine. He was very rarely angry with me, partly because he had not set me up on a pedestal as I had set him, and so was not appalled at finding flaws in my character; partly because he had an intellectual outlet denied to me. But I was often angry with him and we were both living under strains that we did not recognize or understand.

Effie understood. After one of our flare-ups, which were becoming painfully frequent, I found her in tears. This was a rare thing and I was horror-stricken. What was the matter? I had behaved badly to the Man, but surely not to her? What was troubling her so deeply?

How well I remember her answer! "You are spoiling one of the loveliest things in the world."

One of the loveliest things in the world! What did she mean? What was I spoiling? "The Man's and your love for each other."

I have said that Effie was like Shelley. So she was. She had not his unorthodox standards of sexual behaviour, but she was utterly without possessiveness. This was true of her in every way. She had no lust for possessions, she had no care for money, it was the most difficult thing in the world to find for her a Christmas or a birthday present. And now? She had no other thought, no other desire, than that the people she loved should have as far as possible what would make them happiest.

I try to make this clear. Effie was repelled by passion. It frightened her. She shrank instinctively from demands on her which she knew she could not meet without in some obscure way endangering that delicate mental balance which was in her always precarious. Hudson knew this. He told me that he had often tried to make her face life and had been exasperated and angry when she put up a defence against such attempts. People had blamed him for not being "more firm" with her, and he had sometimes blamed himself. But he had come to the conclusion that Effie knew herself better than anyone else did. She knew instinctively how much—or rather how little—she could bear of life without danger. And she fled from it. Sometimes (but this was before I knew her) she would literally flee—lock herself into her room, refuse to come down if there were strangers in the house, and stay till they went away.

She knew herself. She had never (for instance) meant to have a child. She had one and she loved him greatly, but the months of his coming were hell to her and she was out of her mind for two years afterwards. To her, life itself and love that asked too much, were alike terrifying.

There are, nevertheless, few women or men who can face the thought of another giving to the one they love even what they themselves cannot give and do not want. This is where Effie Shaw was apart from the rest of us. She did not wish her husband and her friend to transgress their moral standards or hers: she did want us to have all that was possible for us—not love only, but passionate love.

I marvel as I write it. Will anyone believe that she was never jealous of our love? Perhaps not: yet it is true. She never was. I am certain that she never had to fight against jealousy and never felt it. She was glad that Hudson should have something at least of what he needed: she was glad that I should. She understood our deepest need and met it without effort, with the perfection that can only come from perfect love.

I say that what she gave us met our deepest need. It did so. It did so in spite of all that was denied us.

It is sometimes said that women are more in love with love than a lover. Perhaps it is true. If it is so, then Hudson had something of a woman's quality. He had been twice married, but he had not married a woman capable of passion. His first wife, married very young and dying when their first child was born, seemed almost a shadowy figure to him by now. Perhaps they had never felt more than a rather shadowy affection for each other. Effie was as I have said. And Hudson had now got rooted in his mind the conviction that he was not the sort of man whom a woman could love passionately.

This is always a hard thing for a normal man to bear. It was all the harder for this man because to him passion's fulfilment was most literally a sacrament. It was "the outward and visible sign of an inward and spiritual love". It was, he said to me more than once, with intense feeling, the most dreadful thing that could happen to a man to find that that sacrament, for whose sake he had kept his body as clean as a child's, was to his wife merely "a concession to his lower nature".

He had indeed disciplined his body, but perhaps, in spite of his passionate nature, this had not really been difficult to him. He reverenced passion too much. Unclean thinking was impossible to him and he was innocent in the true sense of the word. He did not know what a prostitute was, he told me, till he went to Oxford and was accosted by one. Both commercial and light "love" were horrible to him, because real passion was so sacred. It was a point on which he felt more strongly and deeply than anyone else I have ever met, and his longing to be passionately loved was not only natural human desire but the longing a man feels for that which he thinks the most beautiful thing on earth.

When Effie asked him to give me something more than friendship, she understood, perhaps without knowing it, his deepest need: she gave him the knowledge that he was one who could be passionately loved.

How strange that he needed such knowledge! It was so easy to love him and I think many women could have loved him so, and perhaps some did though he had no knowledge of it. Women will understand how I loved him. His humility moved me to a passion of tenderness. I could have died to convince him of what seemed to me so obvious a truth—that he was one whom any woman might love wholly, and that it was no lack in him but in them if he had never found the response he hungered for.

He needed that conviction even more than he needed the fulfilment that he could not have. That I gave him and Effie made my giving possible.

From the beginning there were three of us. That made possible everything that was impossible. Hudson and I knew that we must always think of life as including all three. We must never think of any other relationship than this. This was to be our life: Hudson, Effie, and I.

It was not so hard after all. It would indeed have been not hard but simply impossible (being what we were) to have a furtive love affair. How hateful it sounds! Perhaps it should not: there are men and women who do not find it so. This book is not a condemnation or a judgment of others. It is a record of our love—we three. I say only that secrecy to us was impossible. Indeed I never met a being to whom secrecy was so impossible as to Hudson! I often said I hoped life would never make me a fellow-conspirator with him. He was as open as the day and when he tried to be prudent his prudence was like the prudence of an ostrich. It surprised me that so few of our friends guessed that we were more to each other than ordinary friends, but this was not our doing and we never had a "guilty secret" to keep.

This was made possible by Effie. If she had not been what she was we must have parted.

She scolded us when we fell short of the love she imagined for us. She wept when we were angry or ungracious to each other. She made Hudson promise that, if she died, he would marry me "at once"—without waiting—"not troubling about what people said of us". How little we thought how and when we should fulfil her wish! For, whatever she said, we knew that we must never think such thoughts. We must be always three. This was our safety.

I lived with Hudson and Effie for some years. In 1905, when we knew how we loved each other, Hudson gave me a copy of Dante's *Vita Nuova*. I have it still. It is a tiny book, two inches by two and a half. He has marked it here and there. Often he looked back to that year and spoke of it to me as, for him, the beginning of a new life. I believe it was so. On reading some of his letters I believe I have not emphasized enough the wound made in his heart by the failure of his married life in what he regarded as its holiest aspect. This explains the joy he felt in our *Vita Nuova*—as great as mine in spite of the satisfying nature of his work. Years later he wrote:—

"You don't ever regret the Great Day, do you? If you do, try to think of *me*. A veritable *Vita Nuova* it was for me. I was dead with failure, torture, solitariness, sick of life at forty-five, just because the one thing was utterly lacking. Since then, despite all misfortunes . . . I have never been *really* unhappy. *Always, always*, your face has comforted me, your love and trust have raised me up every day. . . . And I wish, oh! how I wish it, that I might have all over again the blessed years that you have given me, from 1901 until now."

From 1901 (the year of our first meeting) until now! The letter is not dated, but it needs no date. He would have written it at any time up to his leaving me in 1944. In another letter, also undated, he writes:—

"Don't I lean upon you, tell you my very soul, take counsel from you, feel absolute trust in you (it never occurs to me to trust you, you are my Other Heart), take life from you, *never enter your presence without a heart-beat, never leave it without a heartbreak*."

So we lived and loved and worked. I soon had as much speaking and lecturing as I could manage—nothing like Hudson's, of course, but for me the strain of working even a slender programme of University Extension from so remote a place as South Luffenham was too great. And work I must. We began to consider the necessity of my leaving them for a more central position, and in the end I went to Oxford for some years.

While there, work even more absorbing came to my help. The fight of Women's Suffrage was quickening. I was swept into it. Soon I had given up lecturing and was speaking almost every day in the week, not always excluding Sunday and often twice a day. The work was terrific. I travelled incessantly and always in third-class carriages. My lameness made everything more tiring. Writing, reading, and generally eating had all to be done in the train. I had hardly time to think. I knew now from experience what the strain of Hudson's life had been, for University Extension was to him what Women's Suffrage was to me. I knew, too, something of the help such work could be. Why do people ever want to deny work to women? How can suffering be borne without it?

In 1907 Hudson accepted the living of Old Alderley in the north of Cheshire. Again, then, at least for a time, we saw more of each other. From Old Alderley it was much easier to work a travelling life and, to our joy (and "our" means all three of us), I could go and live with Hudson and Effie again. Hudson and I were both away a great deal, but Alderley Rectory was our home.

We loved each other more than ever but, in spite of Effie's sympathy and marvellous understanding, Hudson felt a deep uneasiness. Was it right that we should love each other as we did? I thought so: Effie thought so: Hudson was unsure.

At last we agreed that we must separate.

Effie thought us quite mad. It was not in her nature—that very nature that made it possible for her to be what she was to us—to understand the strain life was putting on Hudson and on me. In one way his was the more difficult part for I had no other claim to consider and he had Effie. He could not be sure that it was right for him to give to anyone any part of what, in a perfect marriage, belongs to the wife, even if the marriage was not perfect and what was given to another was only a part. So I accepted his decision. I am not sure even now, but I think I never believed that this was the end. I knew that one reason which weighed heavily with Hudson was nothing to me, and I believed he would realize it as time passed.

This reason was Hudson's belief that if I would put him out of my life I could marry someone else. He dwelt on this often. I was much younger than he. I wanted children and could not have them. If only I would face the break with him, I might.

I could not face it for any other reason than that he wished it and against his wish I had no will in the matter. It is true that I would like to have had children. There are few women, I believe, who would not, though certainly there are some. But there are many women whose wish for children is not only a wish but a passion. These give a greater love to the children they bear than to their husbands, however dear their husbands are. On the other hand, there are women whose love for their husbands is greater than for their children: and there are women—few and great—whose love for all alike is equal. I belong to the second class. I should, I believe, always have loved my husband best. And for me there was only one man in the world. If he might not be my husband no wish for children could make me turn my love to someone else. It seemed to me impossible to the point of absurdity. It didn't even make me angry. I was, I admit, amused when Hudson told me, later, that he would never have let me have children at all because he could never have endured running so great a risk! On this point he was almost morbid, but it was not surprising, considering his experience. His first wife had died in child-birth and his second was driven mad with fear of it. He knew I had not this fear and would certainly have demanded children. I knew he would have desired them, too. Meanwhile I knew and respected his self-reproach when he remembered that, if we had never met, I might have had them.

I went into exile. I had my work. He had his.

After a time he wrote and asked me to come back. Effie, who had never accepted the situation, was delighted. I returned and we never thought of separating again.

We went on working. Oh, blessed work! It is difficult now, except in general terms, to describe what University Extension meant to Hudson and Women's Suffrage to me. Both meant to us a deep faith in democracy, I for women and he for the working-men and women who are the great majority in any country. Put that way, perhaps it will, after all, be understood better now than then, since we have had to fight for it. I must quote one who understood it already, for he was one of the founders of the movement for University Extension and the one who asked Hudson to join it. In 1909 Sir Michael Sadler wrote to Hudson during one of his fits of deep depression:—

"For more than twenty years you have been one of the great moving forces for good in English life. . . . More than any other man you have made Ruskin's words live and bear fruit. You have added much of your own. Like all good interpreters, you are yourself a creator of ideals. Let it be a comfort to you in your illness to think what a great part you have been given to play . . . such influence as you have had comes only to men who give their inmost selves to their work. You have given yourself with a self-lessness that has made your own share in it far less conspicuous than would have been the part of many another man. But those whom you have inspired do not forget and will not forget."

In 1933 he wrote again:—

"Your power of prophecy, like Ruskin's, made you feel that the foundations of habit would be shaken. As if it were yesterday, I hear a note in your voice when you stirred us all to the depths. You have had to bear other people's sorrows through feeling the pain of the world, and it could not be given to you or to anyone to foresee in detail what changes there would be in the minds and moods of the world—so you have had the happiness and the strain of the seer and have been called on to bear the weight of the cloud of depression.

"But I hope you will not forget how much strength you have given to others and that those whom you have encouraged and inspired are thankful for your help and for the moving eloquence of your words. You have been one of the great leaders of our generation and I thank God for you."

By the same post Sir Michael Sadler wrote to me:—

"I must send you thanks for your kindness in letting me know that Mr. Hudson Shaw is ill. I had not heard and am writing to him to-day. He is one of the great leaders of our generation—strong and tender and able to influence men's wills."

A year later he wrote to Hudson again:—

"Wherever you have been you have brought strength and courage and honesty of thinking to all who could understand. God bless you for all you have done."

It is often the lot of those whose work has been that of a teacher to see their reward only in its effect on the lives of their students. If he works with the terrific energy of my husband he has no time to write a book. The impact of his personality remains in the memory of those who had the delight of being taught by him, but those of us who owed him most cannot help but be, perhaps unreasonably, jealous of his fame. Sir Michael Sadler says that it was something "almost mystical", especially among the working-men of the north country. I cannot refrain from putting on record in this book some of the things men said of him—of the man I loved and who loved me.

First, let me say something of the friend who made all this possible to Hudson—Bolton King. This man knew him, only slightly, at Oxford and was deeply impressed. Hearing that, owing to his poverty and his inability to find an opening in this country, Hudson was on the point of accepting an offer to go out to Australia, Bolton King "endowed" him with an income sufficient to make life here possible. Hudson, who felt an over-powering wish to serve the democracy here in the metropolitan country of the empire, was grateful and delighted at this miracle of kindness and accepted without hesitation. He knew his work lay here, and though sometimes almost ludicrously humble about himself he could not doubt his vocation. He wrote:—

December 21st, 1883

To my Unknown Benefactor,

I have longed to write to you, but hardly know how. Thanks and gratitude are difficult to express for such extraordinary generosity as yours to me and I have no words which can adequately tell you what I feel. Only this morning, on receiving your solicitors' communication, have I fully realized all that you are about to do for me. You have given me independence, a career, and hope for the future. . . .

. . . Now, by your wonderful kindness, I shall hope to devote myself with all the strength I have to the work I have always longed for, amongst the poor, and especially the poor of the great cities. I was in despair, and now I am full of hope. . . . I can only promise that, with God's help, I will spend my life in trying to make others happy. One request I have to make, that if ever it be possible and you think it right, I may be allowed to know to whom I owe this opportunity.

G. W. Hudson Shaw.

For years he was not to know. In vain he racked his brains. He had only one friend rich enough to "endow" a poor man and this one friend denied having done so. Bolton King he hardly knew at all and was unaware that he had been watched ever since he had been President of the Oxford Union, where his great powers of speech had made, even among Presidents of that matchless debating society, a great impression. Hudson was prouder of his Presidentship there than of anything else in his life but two. One of these was his election, some years later, to a Balliol Fellowship, which gave him enormous pleasure, for he thought his college the greatest on earth and used to tell me, with many chuckles, that he was the first—and surely the last—man to have this honour without knowing much Latin and with practically no Greek!

At last, Bolton King relented and Hudson learnt who his benefactor was. King had "feared it might make things different between us, but now" (he wrote) "I know it won't. I know you will repay me, so it was the best investment I ever made—the only one of that sort of thing which I look back on with entire content. I feel that if I kept you and your voice for this country, I have done something worth doing and which bears fruit. I don't think you know what you have done or may still do. . . . Now we will never speak or write of it again, and I shall be best pleased if you forget it, only I know you won't."

He never did, and the knowledge that his unknown friend was such a man as Bolton King increased his delight in it. They remained friends to the end of their lives, Hudson even going to the extreme length of *writing* to him—a thing he almost never did to anyone! There is a letter from Bolton King written to Hudson just before his death, sorrowfully endorsed, "Never answered: he died a few days later." But most truly the great debt owed was "repaid", and I think Bolton King never doubted that it was "the best investment" he had ever made. Hudson did all and more than all he promised. Even literally he "repaid" the debt by, in his turn, raising money to send one of his best students, a Lancashire weaver, to Oxford for a university career.

It was, however, an almost impossibly strenuous life that he led. Other parsons have "time off" if they choose to take it: Hudson was working at high speed all the week. Other lecturers could rest on Sundays: Hudson spent his week-end working harder than ever. He *could not* give anyone less than the best that was in him. I have known him mount the pulpit, in his tiny parish church at Luffenham, bursting with eagerness to explain to a congregation of thirty or forty, farmers, farmers' wives, and agricultural labourers, why they need no longer puzzle their brains over the difference in moral elevation between the Book of Deuteronomy and other Books of the Pentateuch. Never having noticed such difference nor puzzled over it for a single instant they sat with unmoved countenance gazing at their remarkable rector. But he was more remarkable even than they knew, for he held them until it seemed that his interest was theirs and they could go home to their Sunday dinners feeling that Deuteronomy was now to them an open book and, moreover, that it was highly important that it should be so. Never in my life have I met anyone who could approach Hudson in ability to teach the humblest scholar without for a moment ceasing to be in the truest sense a scholar himself. He was unique and he remained so to the end.

Sometimes, listening to him, I even regretted that he was a parson. His sermons, though often reaching a height of eloquence and power were not, I thought, so wonderful as his lectures and classes. He, however, was disgusted with me for suggesting this. If he had to live his life over again, he vowed he would be a parson and a parson and a parson to the end of time.

I loved to see Hudson with children. He was at home with them. He had a horrible way of arranging a party to last from, say, 4 p.m. to 7 p.m. As the hour of release drew near, his exhausted helpers' eyes were fixed on the clock, for three hours of Hudson's children's parties were enough to daunt the strongest. At South Luffenham his equipment consisted of (*a*) a large empty barn, and (*b*) a gong. Armed with these, he kept a crowd of children of all ages, from toddlers to teens and beyond, in a state of uproarious festivity, inventing new games and transforming old ones till 7 o'clock.

At seven the gong was banged harder than ever. "Who would like to stay till eight?" Everyone—except the helpers. Uproar ensued.

At 8 p.m. the gong again. "Who would like to stay till nine?" Renewed uproar.

One by one the grown-ups crept away and left Hudson to carry on till midnight. Did he care? He never even noticed.

Why, Effie and I used to ask each other with fury, *why* did Hudson want us to be at these frightful parties if he could do just as well without our help? To this there was no answer, as it was impossible to persuade him that we didn't want to be there. If we thought we didn't, that was our mistake.

From one of his parishes (South Luffenham) a party of men, women, children and Hudson used to start out at 4 a.m., spend a day by the seaside, and return at 4 a.m. next day. This expedition never found Effie and me in the train. We drew the line there. Hudson could never cease to wonder at us. Would we go but *once*, he urged, we would never consent to miss it again. Did we realize that they sang songs all the way there and back, bathed, paddled, ate, drank and went on the switchback or in row-boats the whole day long? We did, and this was why we would not go. Even Hudson could not make us. It was the one point at which he failed and he always knew that the loss was ours.

Years afterwards I remember being in Liverpool Street Station with him when a crowd of mostly elderly women were seen, full of cheer and laughter, making their way to certain reserved carriages in a part of the train bound for some sea-side resort. Hudson paused and looked longingly at them. "It must be a Mothers' Outing," he whispered to me with a hungry look in his eyes. For two pins he would have joined up and gone with them. I didn't offer him even one and he let them depart with a sigh—such a genuine sigh.

It didn't matter what kind of a bean-feast it was: Hudson

was all for it. Men, women, and children—he was always completely unself-conscious and completely at home.

It was a point on which Effie never tried and I never succeeded in feeling at one with him. We raged at him when he dragged us in, or tried to. We laughed when he failed. Effie and I always laughed at the same things. So, with her perfect trust and our engrossing work, we lived and loved, and it was not too hard.

For to me, too, work that demanded all I had to give came in plenty, and I think it was his own delight in his own exacting toil that made Hudson so sympathetic with me. He never grudged me to my cause. It would be rather less than honest to claim that he was a soundly saved feminist! He would sometimes enrage me and surprise his friends by a sudden reversion to the ideals of *Sesame and Lilies*; but as far as I personally was concerned he had no limitations. Nothing was too great for me—no conditions, no limitations were to bar my way.

Never shall I forget what he said to me once, after a meeting in the Queen's Hall at which I had made what he thought a great speech. As we went home together he said— "Even if we had been able to marry, it would have been a crime for me to marry you. You don't belong to any man; you belong to the world."

Of course, we would have married if we could. We both knew that. Yet it is very dear to me to know that he could think of me so, even for a moment. And it was because he could and did that we were able to live and love as we did and find it not too hard.

There are other men and women who have lived and loved as we did. I know some of them. I salute them here. We would not, in the end, have had it otherwise. He, as he said, "only loved me". I only loved him. Can anyone ask more of life than that? To me it *was* life to be loved as he loved me. To him the same.

It was in 1907 that Hudson went to Old Alderley. I think

he was conscious of a greater response from his people there than in any other parish and, reading the letters that belong to this period, I wish it might have been longer.

Alderley, like South Luffenham, is a country parish and Hudson loved the country; but it was near to great centres of population, being on the fringe of Lancashire. This made University Extension work easier and lessened the burden of travelling. Besides this, it was easier for people to come to him, and for the first time in his life Hudson had the joy of a crowded church and responsive congregation. Elsewhere his influence as a preacher had been greater and deeper than he could ever be got to realize, but at Old Alderley he could be in no doubt.

It is interesting to know that Mrs. Humphry Ward, who was a friend of the Stanleys and sometimes stayed at Alderley Park, even hoped that Hudson might be the leader of the reform described in her most famous novel, *Robert Ellesmere*. She had attended Alderley church, found it crowded, and in a letter to a friend quoted with approval Hudson's words : "I shall not in future read the Athanasian Creed, or the cursing psalms or the Ten Commandments, or the Exhortation at the beginning of the Marriage Service—and I shall take the consequences. The Baptismal Service ought to be altered—so ought the Burial Service. And how you, the laity, can tolerate us—the clergy—standing up Sunday after Sunday and saying these things to you, I cannot understand. But I for one will do it no more, happen what may."

Hudson never wavered from this decision and continually brought the matter to the attention of his people. He was before his time, not in thinking these things but in the boldness with which he proclaimed them when others were silent. But he was far too orthodox for Mrs. Humphry Ward's neo-Unitarianism and his views, so boldly preached at Alderley, aroused great interest. When he left Old Alderley for London, he left with reluctance a truly responsive congregation.

His successor in the living, Rev. C. B. Welland, wrote of him:—

"George William Hudson Shaw brought to Alderley the gift of his brilliant mental powers. Alderley church was soon well known to large numbers of people who lived outside the parish. In the time of Canon Bell, evensong had been changed from an afternoon to an evening service, and now both morning and night the church was frequently crowded. He was not only an attractive preacher. An enthusiast for beauty and bright colour, he laboured to adorn the buildings which had come within his trust. The School was recently gone from the churchyard to another place, and Lord Sheffield prepared and presented a Hall and Room for the use of the parish. Mr. Shaw would have nothing on their walls but the pictures that are excellent. In the church, curtain and carpet had to be supreme in hue and design. Anything that was unsightly, whatever its virtue in being old, was considered unfit for Alderley church. In Mr. Shaw's mind, this was a principle of the highest importance. Worship should be in a fair place.

"In many ways the parish felt itself renewed. Men's clubs were established in Alderley and Warford. A Library was opened on Sundays in the Parish Hall. Long before the rule was universal in the English church, Alderley had its Church Council. In the Hall the people went to dance."

I cannot refrain from adding that, like many great democrats, Hudson expected his Church Council to agree with him and, of course, it did. But he also established the election of the May Queen by the children themselves and they were not always so amenable. I regret to say that the rector thought May Queens should be as pretty (at least) as they were good. When the children elected a girl whose merits were greater than her beauty, he was outraged. He *all but* dis-allowed the election—not quite, however. This was a great victory and I believe only children could have won it.

Hudson was so superb a teacher that, as I have said, I sometimes grudged him to other work. He seemed to me to be greater as a lecturer than a preacher and his sermons best when they were teaching sermons. But to him his work as a preacher and pastor was dearest of all. Never for one instant of his life had he wished himself a layman.

Since his death I have been going through his diaries. Some are lost, some have gaps of months, some, especially after his retirement, contain more entries about the state of his garden than anything else. Occasionally, though rarely, he has not noted dates of importance to me: but never have I failed to find a note of the fact that he was ordained on Trinity Sunday, with the number of years that have passed since then.

So at Alderley he was happy, except for the terrible times of depression which first struck him when an undergraduate at Oxford and never completely left him till his death.

I have not spoken of these hours of darkness before. Hudson fought against them like a lion. Indeed some of his sermons and lectures delivered when he was thus spiritually tormented were the most lion-like of any I heard. He turned his pain into a challenge that stirred his hearers to the depths, whether they knew (as Effie and I did) what he was suffering or were ignorant of it. At such times he could be terrible.

But at what a cost! I don't know how much of his depression was physical and how much due to the strain of his life and his work. No doubt the constant travelling in great discomfort, with irregular meals and late nights, was largely to blame. Hudson would travel all day, lecture in the afternoon, go to the home of one of his admirers and friends, lecture again in the evening, allow the class held afterwards to go on as long as students demanded, and go back to absorbing conversations with host and hostess till long after midnight. Often he had no food till nine or ten o'clock.

THE JOLLY MILLER

THERE WAS A JOLLY MILLER
LIVED ON THE RIVER DEE,.......
AND THIS THE BURDEN OF HIS SONG
FOREVER ....   SEEMED TO BE,.....

"I CARE FOR NOBODY, NO, NOT I,
AND NOBODY CARES
FOR ME."......

LEAGUE OF NATIONS

CITY CHURCHES

WOMENS MINISTRY

L OF N PILGRIMAGE

S. BOTOLPHS

Drawing by Effie Shaw of her husband—with apologies to his congregation! Effie always held that they endured far too patiently his many
enthusiasms and should have called a halt, such as the meditative beast
in the picture is evidently considering. Had the drawing been made a
few years later, the work of Dr. Schweitzer would certainly have been
added to the other "causes" and would perhaps have been the greatest
of all.

Then he would, exhausted, eat an enormous meal (Eat it? bolt it, I should say) and either continue talking into the small hours or go straight to bed; either course being equally destructive to digestion.

Hudson enjoyed this mad way of living and was perhaps too temperamental to work in any other way. But he paid for it. And only too often he came home not only to his parson's job of visiting and preaching, but to a wife as temperamental and more fragile than he, in one of her times of mental trouble.

He had an iron constitution and extraordinary vitality. Naturally Effie, who had neither, hung upon him. Just as she could not understand why conversation was impossible if she never responded, so she took it for granted that Hudson, however exhausted, would always protect and sustain her. His very muscle was a joy to her. Once, when in one of her acute accesses of fear, she asked him "what he would do if a policeman came to take her away?" "Smash his face in", was the prompt reply, and even in her misery Effie could not help laughing. She was so sure he could.

But this robust muscular force of body and energy of character was accompanied by a most sensitive mind, and Hudson endured tortures of depression as terrible as Effie's periods of fear. I wonder whether they would have been less terrible if he had not fought so hard against them. But that was impossible. He could not relax, for he had to earn a living for Effie, himself, and his two sons. Lecture he must and lecture he did, in blood and sweat.

Perhaps he could not have lived otherwise than he did in any case. He worked with fury because he was like that. And he, at least, never faltered and never complained. It was I, looking on, who suffered—and who did complain, but without effect, except on myself. Effie understood better than I, perhaps, how futile it was to try to curb his spirit. She made no attempt to do so. I beat my head against the stone wall of his mind and only broke my heart against it.

There are few pains worse than the pain of standing by and watching someone you love destroying himself. I watched this, as I thought, for years. It seems futile now, for Hudson lived to be eighty-five and worked till he was seventy-five, and so can hardly be said to have "destroyed himself". Yet he did pay a terrible cost in suffering which might—only *might*—have been less if he had lived differently.

Of one thing I am devoutly thankful: I did not fray his nerves or temper by my protests for he paid no more heed to them than he did to my carefully considered advice about organ-stops! He took not the slightest notice of advice from anybody or at any time, though no one was more earnest in asking for it. Exasperating man! In Chesterton's words—"he chose his path and went down it like a thunder-bolt".

CHAPTER IV

In 1912 we moved to London. Hudson was offered the living of St. Botolph's, Bishopsgate, and we went, together as a matter of course, to live in a London flat in Bedford Square.

Effie liked London. The curious impersonality of London life suited her. She felt unwatched, unnoticed, anonymous. I cannot remember her suffering from any terrors while we were in Bedford Court Mansions, though, on the other hand, I think she retreated more and more into herself and that shadowy existence in which she could hardly be said to live. We no longer had days of happy companionship in country drives or in the garden. In London I worked more furiously than ever and Hudson, though he gave up Extension lecturing, disappeared into his church and parish for whole days. It was perhaps a good thing that we were not long in our flat.

An aged aunt came to be added to Hudson's household.* He moved out to the Hampstead Garden Suburb and in his new house, with the aunt, there was not room for me except for visits. A larger house could not be afforded. I was constantly with them as a visitor and we took our holidays together, but my home now was in Poplar.

The war began. Hudson, bursting with enthusiasm, appeared in khaki, wearing the uniform of a chaplain to the H.A.C., in which his son Bernard had enlisted. Few colonels looked so much like a colonel as Hudson. His white collar and tie were completely unconvincing. He seemed to have put them on by mistake. Going to look for him in the lounge of the Great Eastern Hotel, a stranger, who had an appointment with him, came away disappointed. "There

* On her death, Effie's mother (Hudson's aunt) joined them.

was no parson there," he explained later—"only an officer." Nothing, perhaps, but his Balliol fellowship ever gave Hudson greater delight than his chaplaincy. He enjoyed preaching to his lambs in uniform more than to any other congregation.

One Easter Sunday, when he had preached with all his force and fire on Immortality, one of the officers—a real colonel—remarked that he had no belief or wish for a life after death. "I have often noticed", said Hudson, with complete absence of guile, "that people who haven't much vitality find it difficult to believe in eternal life." He was surprised to see his colonel transfixed with rage. To be told by a mere chaplain that his intellectual doubts were due to lack of vitality nearly caused him to put the matter to the test at once by bursting a blood-vessel.

Hudson was a very male man and had many men friends —more than most men, I think, or at least more faithful. In spite of his infamous record as a correspondent, his friends never ceased to be his friends and those who loved him loved him always. Nor did he lose his power of making new ones. When later in life he went down to live in the country he found himself next door to Dr. Frederick Mosely, and when he had a heart attack Dr. Mosely came to the rescue. At once they were friends and their only quarrel was whether Hudson should or should not be allowed to pay this doctor-friend any fee. Later he got into trouble with his teeth, and his dentist, the famous Warwick James, became another much-loved friend. In after years Warwick (who was my friend also) wrote that Hudson had "added a certain poetry to his action and thought". Dr. Mosely wrote to me later: "I loved him terribly". Ah, terribly—yes, we loved him terribly.

Most wonderful of all to me was the tribute of his distinguished brother, Dr. Batty Shaw. Dr. Shaw was a great man, but in so different a way that understanding between them seemed almost impossible. Yet he wrote in 1935, on hearing of Hudson's resignation from St. Botolph's:—

"Leaving my hospital work is a trifle in comparison, for though no longer may I look after the bodies of God's poor, you are to give up the care of that which is imperishable. Impossible! As long as you live and for long after, thousands will be saying that you have been to them a mainstay. No wonder. In spite of grievous physical impediments you have gone on longer than many more comfortably balanced embodiments of energy and zeal—and yet have been effective."

Wonderful as this tribute is, coming from a brother himself brilliant, but in so different a way from Hudson, it is yet not so moving as another from his elder son Arnold—the child of his first wife. This son was like Hudson in many ways, not least in his personal charm, but he had not the strength of character which underlay his father's temperamental gifts. In some ways, therefore, he could hardly help disappointing him, and while still very young he went out to America, married and settled down there. Unfortunately, it happened that Hudson never visited the U.S.A. after this, though he was always planning to. Arnold, however, came to England with his wife and little daughter and this was a great happiness to them all. Indeed it was such happiness that it seems tragic that Hudson did not again visit America. He had been there several times on lecture tours that were spectacularly successful, but the claims on his time and strength at home made further absences impossible. Nor could Arnold get across to England. But their love for each other remained unbroken. Arnold was easily influenced by the people he was with. He had become a Roman Catholic after his meeting with his first wife who was of that communion. He worked as lecture-agent for John Cowper Powys. Both influenced him deeply: but no one ever weakened Hudson's influence. Arnold writes of the "overflowing of his heart" in thankfulness "that you above all men are my father" and his longing "that my dear father could see just a little of himself in me". It is a tribute from a son that any father might envy.

They were indeed in many ways alike, and above all in their common passion for social justice and pity for the oppressed. It was this that was their bond of union: it was this, I do not doubt, that made Hudson love his elder son with an intensity which, he confessed to me, was of a different quality and depth from that which he felt for the younger—Effie's son Bernard—fond and proud of him too though he was. Arnold "suffered all his life for everyone ground under the heel of the merciless economic system", which was in the United States at that time even more merciless than here. Hudson suffered in the same way and was able to speak out his compassion and to give his whole strength to the business of relieving this exploitation by giving the knowledge which is power to its victims. Arnold could not do this, had no outlet for his pity, and suffered the more; but all who knew them both could see that there was truly "something of his father" in the son and that this was an abiding joy to both.

In later years it was Albert Schweitzer whose friendship meant most of all to Hudson, and on this I must dwell a little longer. I need not speak of the power and genius of this great man. Hudson was one of the first in this country to acclaim him. What was, to me, so glorious was the instant sympathy and understanding between these two men. It was to Hudson himself a crowning glory.

On one occasion, when appealing for money for Dr. Schweitzer's work, he flung his very old and much-loved gold watch into the collection. Afterwards realizing that this was not half what he wanted to give he asked to be allowed to "ransom" it. Schweitzer promised that he should have it back "in a few days". It came—with an inscription inside and with this little note:—

"DEAR FRIEND,
I asked for your watch to have the following in-

scribed. Open it and you will find it. Wear this watch with this inscription in which we are united."

The inscription ran:

"Rev. Hudson Shaw et Dr. Albert Schweitzer
Fratres.
21.5.28."

This watch had always been dear to Hudson because it was given him by his students at an American University Extension centre in Germantown, Philadelphia. It was now the most precious possession he had. When, in the passage of time, it grew old and would not register time at all, he had it on his bedside table and never parted from it till a few days before his death. He then gave it to me and I took it away, but the next day he said he couldn't sleep without it and demanded it back. He had it and I have it now. What man in the world would not be proud to be called "Brother" by Albert Schweitzer? Brother and friend.

"Dr. Schweitzer was deeply moved that you came to Liverpool Street Station in the evening" (to see him off on the journey) "and he is so thankful to you for your kind words and your personal letter. When the train went off he said to me with emotion, when he spoke of you, that it is a great thing for him to have you as his friend."*

Hudson certainly earned this proud title and I had the joy of sharing his immense respect for this great man. There was a friendly rivalry between St. Botolph's congregation and the Guildhouse as to which should do more for his Lambarene hospital. On the whole I think the Guildhouse won! We built the ward for mental patients and sank the well that their hospital water supply should not fail. St. Botolph's, at the doctor's request, gave him the lamp to light his patients to the hospital quay when coming down the river in search

* Emma Hauskrecht, letter to G.W.H.S. from Alsace, dated December 9th, 1936.

of him through the darkness of the tropical nights; and endowed it with money enough to keep it burning. It bore the
inscription:

"Here, at whatever hour you come, you will find light
and help and human kindness."

I linger over memories like these, running far ahead of the
story of our love as I have written it, because it is a joy to do
so, but also because they show a little the sort of man it was
who gave me his love.

Things that seem humanly impossible are more to be
understood when seen in the light of all that Hudson was
doing, all that he was to hundreds, thousands, of others.

I turn over the leaves of his diaries. They are hardly more
than entries of his various engagements, but what a record!
I have suggested that he never received from any parish the
same response that he did from the people of Old Alderley.
That is true as regards his congregation: he never succeeded
in filling St. Botolph's. It takes someone with other gifts
perhaps, and certainly with better physical health, to bring
any congregation at all to a London City church, and St.
Botolph's was at least one of the best, until Hudson's increasing ill-health made his being able to preach on any given
date uncertain. But this refers only to Sundays. During the
week the church was enormously active. To Hudson alone
surely would it have occurred to have a May Queen crowned
in the heart of the City of London—generally in June and
once even, I believe, in July, but what of that? Hudson
scorned to be bound by calendars. It was he, too, who
turned part of the graveyard into a tennis-court which was
such a joy that another City rector eagerly wrote to ask him
"how on earth he had got a faculty for it?" To which the
answer was, "I wasn't such a fool as to ask."

Had he lived only a little longer, a swimming-pool would
have been built somewhere—under the tennis-court or the

parish room or the church—I don't know and he never explained, but in any case no doubt without a faculty.

I never met anyone who could adduce such splendid reasons for doing what he wanted as Hudson. But then what he wanted to do was fine and great. His real gift to his people was not any sensational novelty but his weekly, monthly, yearly teaching. There were many clubs and classes at St. Botolph's, and the best of all and dearest to him was "the Friday Class", which met weekly at midday to study theology under his guidance. It is not too much to say he *adored* this class. All the enthusiasm and fire of the old University Extension lecturing days went into his work there. And all his reading. He could "take the guts" out of a book quicker than any reader I ever met. He read, re-read, annotated, boiled down, and produced for his students what they longed to know. I believe that even they would be amazed if they could see the records of books read, the hours of reading, the research, that were his preparation for his class or congregation. He was not in the technical sense a scholar, having little Latin, less Greek, and no Hebrew at all; but what a scholarly mind he had! There are notes of his reading in preparation for preaching or teaching which show his enormous capacity for taking pains, combined with an equally enormous gusto in sharing the result. He couldn't help sharing. To the end of his life the subject that was engrossing his own attention was offered with staggering enthusiasm to all and sundry. He aroused the interest of his charwomen in the origins of the Gospels and detained for two hours an unfortunate visitor—a complete stranger who had come to ask if he might have half a dozen goldfish from Hudson's well-stocked pond—with reasons for assigning the Fourth Gospel to this author or that. Years before, he astonished a railway platform crowded with travellers by throwing up the window of his carriage as the train drew out and roaring to the stationmaster with whom he had been conversing—"Have you got the Everlasting Mercy?" He

"ATTRACTIVE" AND "PRESENTABLE" CLOTHES FOR PARSONS (CONTINUED.)

THE FREE CHURCH

FULHAM PALACE.

THE GARDEN SUBURB.

ARE YOU A SOCIALIST: IF NOT - WHY NOT

NOTICE: W.E.A. MEETING H.G.S.

FOR THE SUMMER MEETING.

FOR RE-UNION TO MEET NONCONFORMISTS

FOR COURT WEAR. OR TRADES UNION USE.

TO FULHAM.

FOR THE MOTHERS' UNION.

FOR THE ALLOTMENTS.

FOR GARDEN PARTIES.

"BISHOPS SHOULD MAKE THEIR CLERGY ATTRACTIVE AND PRESENTABLE." REV. B.G. BOURCHIER. PARISH. MAG. H.G.S.

Effie Shaw was delighted by the statement made by the Vicar of St. Jude's, Hampstead Garden Suburb, to the effect that the clergy should be made "attractive and presentable". She here suggests that the next issue of the Parish Magazine should contain instructions on this point. [The Vicar at that time was the Rev. B. G. Bourchier.]

meant Masefield's poem, just published, and an instant success with him. He could not leave the stationmaster in ignorance of it for a whole day.

Hudson read enormously and remembered what he read. He fell upon a subject and tore the heart out of it. At one time it was the acutely controversial subject of the suffering of God. This is perhaps still controversial in another Communion than ours.* Hudson found in it a satisfying answer to the problem of human suffering in the first World War. He set to work to collect a long list of the theologians and Church dignitaries who believed that God Himself suffered with us in our agony. It contained the names of an impressive number of these, but also at least one which was not impressive at all. For some reason Hudson was specially delighted with this one and called on me to rejoice.

"But, Hudson, that man can't have an opinion. He hasn't the brains of a rabbit."

"N-no—but he is a Bishop!"

At one time Hudson was in transports of delight at the discovery of the ancient manuscript known as the *Codex Sinaiticus*, which was eventually bought by the British Museum. It was on view to the public there and Hudson could not keep away. The Codex, for some reason, excited almost as much interest in a large number of completely ignorant people as in Hudson himself, and long queues passed daily along the place of exhibition. Hudson saw it again and again and observed with a thrill that it lay open at a certain passage in St. Luke's Gospel which specially interested him. Of course, he soon saw that most of the queue-ers knew nothing of its importance and their blank silence or ignorant surmises awoke his teaching soul. He was unable to refrain from explaining the matter to those nearest to him in the queue. Soon they were fully informed of the discovery and the discoverer, the nature of a Codex,

* The Roman Catholic: I believe Hudson's view is definitely condemned as heretical in the Church of Rome.

the importance of this one and the special significance of the passage exposed to view. Others gathered round. The queue became a class. The class grew into a crowd. Everyone was entranced and all eyes were fastened upon the lecturer or the exhibit. It was with the utmost difficulty that the "class" was dispersed by the Museum officials, and I thought nothing but police with drawn truncheons would have succeeded.

Hudson was delighted. He explained the matter of the *Codex Sinaiticus* to me a hundred times and we ate a luncheon together about it in some City hall. Infected with his enthusiasm I appealed to my Guildhouse congregation for a collection to help the British Museum's fund for purchase. But I was not Hudson and failed to interest them in the least. They thought £100,000 could easily be spent on something more useful and the collection was meagre. Hudson and I were bitterly disappointed, but consoled each other, especially when it was made known that the whole amount had been given or promised. We went to two theatres and Frascati's Restaurant to celebrate this.

At another time I was fascinated by the studies of anthropologists and tried to interest Hudson. He was not to be stirred. Theology, yes: history, yes: anthropology, definitely no. I plodded along by myself, and one Saturday he took up one of the books I was reading to see what on earth I was so interested in. Suddenly he took fire. He seized my books, ordered a lot more, ate them up and produced the most marvellous diagrams, genealogical trees and the like, to illustrate their meaning. His "Friday Class"—he was rector of St. Botolph's at the time—was switched from St. Luke and the Authorship of the Fourth Gospel to Pithecanthropus and Piltdown Man with the same consuming ardour as that which drew a crowd round the *Codex Sinaiticus*. I had not in years acquired, nor could I ever have handled, the material which Hudson mastered and marshalled in a few months.

Then he returned with gusto to a study of the Book of Job. We read it together.

"The end of this book is an anticlimax," he declared. "Some other hand must have added it."

"I suppose so," said I, "but it is not an anticlimax. It is the answer that the Psalmist gave to the mystery of human suffering when he wrote—'Then thought I to understand these things but they were too hard for me: until I went into the sanctuary of God.' * That is the answer."

"It is no answer," he said.

We argued about it all that morning, but we didn't convince each other. Perhaps we very rarely did. It was not by convincing arguments that we were drawn so close together but by a common interest and delight in discussion. We lit each other up.

* Psalm 73, verses 16 and 17.

CHAPTER V

THOUGH IT was a lasting disappointment to Hudson that his great church was not filled on Sundays, his life at St. Botolph's was a happy one. To understand how our love for one another stood the strain of incompletion, and grew always stronger, it is necessary to remember this. He had, as always, terrible periods of depression which interrupted his work; but he was still as full of energy and gusto when well as ever in his life. London with its roaring streams of life suited and inspired him. I am convinced that he would have crowded his church but for the long interruptions of ill-health and consequent uncertainty about his being able to preach.

It was too much to expect people to travel to the heart of the City of London on Sunday mornings when all means of transport were at their lowest point, on the bare chance of hearing a man they would willingly have travelled far to hear if he had not been forced, again and again, to disappoint them. But during the week, when the City was seething with life, St. Botolph's seethed also and reflected the vitality of its rector. Above all, the Friday Class grew into something more than a class; it was a fellowship. Dr. Horton, who sometimes visited it, said it "resembled a group of the Primitive Church". One student writes:—

"Unfortunately I cannot recall all the interesting features of my early association with W.H.S. and St. Botolph's—it goes back into the misty past! I know we used to meet on Friday evenings in the Vestry, and when I first attended the class I believe we studied the growth of Islam. When the class grew and met at lunch-time in the parish room the rector, out of the fullness of his knowledge, led us into many fields of research and exploration, *e.g.*, comparative religious testimony (Eddington and Jeans), etc. But the main field of study and exploration was the "New Bible" (as W.H.S. called it), especially Gospel origins (with Canon Streeter as guide).

"We have had some wonderful seasons of fellowship. I remember a most gracious retreat we had on a certain Good Friday. I also remember the furore created when the rector secured Miss Royden (as she was then known) to occupy his pulpit on a Good Friday many years ago.

"Of course the Friday Class was unique and comprised in its membership Methodists, Congregationalists, Spiritualists, Baptists, as well as Anglicans (High and Low).

"I have been searching among my papers for an extract from one of the old Church Magazines where W.H.S. set out the main points of his teaching, but alas ! without success. I cannot remember all the points, but they included:—

1. The passibility (capable of feeling or suffering) of God.
2. The influence of the band of women on the New Testament writers (especially St. Luke).
3. The New Astronomy, etc., etc."

Here is the tribute of another student:—

"Mr. Shaw was one of those fine intellectual men who, possessing great knowledge, was able to impart that knowledge in an amazing way. He was exceedingly well read, and kept himself very much abreast of modern knowledge of the Bible. His Thursday services in St. Botolph's were always challenging and inspiring, and his Friday Class was a very great fellowship that he built up. And I am quite sure that many members of that class owe a great deal of their knowledge of the Bible and the literature connected with it as a result of their meeting with him."

I, too, was happy in those days. The first World War had made me a pacifist and on this point Hudson could not agree with me, but our love never depended on agreement and it grew and deepened year by year. I think it was all the more joyful in that we enjoyed the clash of mind on mind. We were born arguers all our lives. And on the main points we were, after the war, happily working together. I preached often at St. Botolph's and Hudson at the Guildhouse.

The incident referred to by one of his students with regard to the Three Hours Service on Good Friday created a fantastic stir at the time. Hudson wished me to conduct it in 1919, but the Bishop intervened. He said that the whole question of the Ministry of Women in the Church of England was coming before the Lambeth Conference and while he, the Bishop, was strongly in favour of permission being given to women to preach, it would prejudice the case if, in the meantime, the clergy in his diocese acted in a disorderly way. Hudson (and I also) saw the point of this and, though deeply disappointed, obeyed Dr. Winnington-Ingram's order and held the service in the Parish Room. I said exactly the same things to exactly the same people—except that many couldn't get in—as if we had been in the church, but that we were not in the church apparently made all the difference.

We awaited events. The Lambeth Conference met and reported in favour of women preaching in church "at non-statutory services". Still we waited. Nothing came from the Bishop. Finally, in 1923, Hudson again asked leave for me to take the Three Hours Service and again the Bishop forbade him. Hudson went off to reason with him. Dr. Winnington-Ingram admitted that the rector had a legal right to invite me to his pulpit for a non-statutory service. He admitted that the Three Hours Service was non-statutory. He admitted that the Lambeth Conference had done exactly what he had asked us to wait for and had affirmed the right of women to preach in church. But no woman could be allowed to take

THE WISDOM OF CANTERBURY.

NOT FOR MEN.

The Lambeth Conference decided that women might preach at non-statutory services and "normally to women and children only". The question arose—what did "normally" mean in this connection? And if men insisted on entering the church would they be abnormal? Or brawlers? The names here are nearly all of women who preached at St. Botolph's at Hudson's invitation. Mrs. Creighton did not. Dame Henrietta Barnett did repeatedly. Miss Carta Sturge preached on Spiritual Healing (in which Effie had no faith): hence the gibe at "Toothache and Prayer".

the Three Hours Service *because it was a specially sacred service.*

At this Hudson broke loose. Up to the point he—who really loved his Bishop—was open to reason and willing to discuss the matter: but to be told that a woman might not preach at a service because it was a sacred one got him on the raw. He came to me raging and asked if I would agree to defy the Bishop and hold the service in St. Botolph's church. I did. Truth to tell, I was as much outraged as he. Had I been refused on the score of my personal unfitness for so sacred an occasion I would, God knows, have felt the reasonableness of the objection. But to be refused because I was a woman was what I could not consent to, and surely all women would have felt joy, as I did, in Hudson's indignant rejection of such a command. But was he not bound to obey his Bishop? "Only", said Hudson firmly, "in his godly admonitions and godly judgments:* this is not godly—not at all."

The service was held. The church was crowded. There was no disturbance or interruption. Hudson, however, became something of an outcast in the diocese and was shouted down when he tried to speak at a subsequent diocesan conference. I observed ruefully—"You'll never be a bishop", and he said he didn't want to be. He didn't. I never knew a man more indifferent to ambition of this kind, or more ambitious of doing the work he was doing to the highest pitch of his great ability.

He did it. In reply to certain charges brought, quite reasonably, against some of the City churches, he set out a statement of the state of things at St. Botolph's, Bishopsgate, in his parish magazine, in 1933. It claims 81,200 attendances at religious services and classes during the year; 40,000 using the church for silent worship and prayer; 7,820 attendances at "Parish Room activities, Sunday School Classes, Women's Meetings", etc. It is a great record and it was

* See the service for the Ordering of Priests, in the Anglican Prayer-book.

achieved in the face of physical fatigue and frequent periods of black depression.

In spite of these, Hudson was happy and absorbed in his work. It was his salvation. So was it mine. I was now at the Guildhouse and my life was very full. We had all manner of people there, most of them people it was interesting to meet and to hear. I had enthusiastic colleagues. Our work met with a great response. The building was used for all it was worth and indeed more, for one member of our Committee was anxious to hold meetings in "a small room" which on enquiry turned out to be a large cupboard; another was shocked to find that no use was being made of part of our roof, which happened to be flat; and the whole church insisted on turning our small paved yard into a garden and holding "garden-parties" there after services on Sunday evenings.

Hudson came to preach sometimes and held classes for Bible study. It was a wonderful time for us both and we lived our lives to the full extent of our powers.

There was only one cloud in our sky. Effie was unhappy.

Life in the Hampstead Garden Suburb did not offer the same anonymity as Bedford Square. People were expected to be neighbourly and Effie could never accept this claim. Once more she became a prey to fear, and often she could only be partly reassured even by Hudson's presence. Their home, besides, was now even farther from his parish than Bedford Square had been. Hudson disappeared into the City in the morning and was away till evening fell or later. Effie suffered paroxysms of terror and rang him up continually, begging him to come back at once. Even in the middle of a service a message would come imploring his return. She couldn't say because she didn't know what frightened her: it was life itself. And the strain on Hudson was very great.

On the other hand, Effie did, at intervals, venture out a little and even made some friends. Her circle widened and we saw—between her terrors—the old gaiety and peculiar charm that was always hers. It even survived the terrible shock of her son's death in 1917. Bernard was dear to her as only sons are dear to mothers, and more *necessary* to her than to others, because of the extreme narrowness of her range. She bore the loss in silence and without the comfort of a "sure and certain hope" of reunion. I have a letter Hudson wrote to her eight years later, when he had been ordered to Switzerland for a rest:—

"I have not forgotten what day it is; your own heart will assure you of that. It was the last thing I thought of last night, the first when I awoke. *His* death-day! Eight years ago since you and I endured the one great catastrophe of our married life and you bore it with such heart-rending courage.

"We seem to have a secret compact not to speak of Bernard together and to keep his day in silence. . . . I respect what I guess is your instinct. Hard enough to bear in silence: too hard if one spoke to the other of the wound which does not, never in this world will heal.

"Sometimes I feel as though I *could* not endure it any longer, as if thought about that young life with its harsh cutting off would drive one out of one's mind. All so senseless, so apparently sacrifice in vain. . . . And it is harder for you than for me. He was very near to you, to you only I think. There is *no* tie so binding as sonship.

"I only want you to know as the years pass . . . that I am profoundly thinking of our one child, always *proud* and glad of him with his sweet and noble nature, with that humorous gurgling laugh of his that I can hear this moment, and prouder still of your stoic courage. Some day I hope that to that stoic bravery will be added the sure and certain Christian hope that he lives still and we shall meet him again, somehow, somewhere."

Effie survived. She could not speak and suffered the more, finding no relief. I never knew—nor did anyone—what

Effie believed, nor even whether she looked forward to meeting her son again in another world. She would not, she could not, speak of these things, and endured life with, apparently, no better armour than fine stoicism. As, in her last years, she was to suffer pain from rheumatism that must often have been acute without complaint, so now she gave no expression to her grief, even to Hudson. She was intensely proud of Bernard, whose death in action, leading his men, was the tragic but glorious consequence of his own self-sacrifice. At a time when the mortality among the younger commissioned officers was such that an appeal had to be made to the non-commissioned to apply for a commission on grounds of the urgent need for them, Bernard obeyed the call and volunteered. In a few weeks he was killed. He had regarded his commission as equivalent to a death-warrant. He was only one of thousands who felt the same, who acted as he did, and were as brave as he; but every mother of those thousands must have burned with pride in her son's self-sacrifice. So did Effie, and all the more because Bernard was so large a part of her narrow world. Yet she said nothing.

How then do I know what she felt? In a way so strange that it could not have happened to anyone on earth but Effie.

She left behind her a number of letters written to her few friends telling how proud she was of her son and how she tried to be as brave as he was so that she might have a right to be proud. Those letters, I am quite sure, were never sent. They are not copies: what could be the purpose of making copies? There are no answers to them and Effie would surely have kept such answers if she had had any. Her writing them and not sending them was only one more instance of the extraordinary inhibition which, while it demanded some self-expression—some outlet of feeling—never allowed that self-expression to reach the world. Her pride and her grief poured itself out in these letters. No one saw them till after her death. All those to whom she wrote them are now

MY HOUSE IN HAMPSTEAD

I lived there from 1919 till I went to live next door to the
Old Cottage, in 1935.

SOUTH LUFFENHAM RECTORY

Church spire at a distance behind. The church is a very lovely specimen of Early English architecture. One aisle is Roman.

THE HUDSON SHAWS' HOUSE IN THE HAMPSTEAD GARDEN SUBURB

A Lutyens building.

ST. BOTOLPH'S, BISHOPSGATE: *interior*

The church is in the Wren style, with large galleries and a high pulpit. When I preached the "Three Hours" here angry objectors threatened to throw me out of it.

ST. BOTOLPH'S, BISHOPSGATE

Hudson Shaw was rector here from 1913 till his retirement.
The churchyard was the scene of his May Queen Festival
(usually held in June) and part of it was laid out as a
tennis-court for City workers. (The trees had to be cut
down afterwards as they were diseased. This was after
Hudson's death.)

THE OLD COTTAGE, BAYLEY'S HILL, SEVENOAKS

An almost perfect example of a red-roofed, red-tiled, 14th-century Kentish building. Hudson and Effie Shaw retired here before his resignation from St. Botolph's. I lived

STUDY IN THE GARDEN OF THE OLD COTTAGE

Hudson Shaw built this, overlooking the Weald of Kent. It is so faithful to the traditions of Kentish building as to be indistinguishable in style from the cottage itself. Behind it was a little wooden bridge leading into the bluebell wood of which Hudson said that heaven was like that. The view from the door of the study is shown in another picture.

THE KENTISH WEALD

This photograph was taken from inside the study whose
door-way frames the picture. The ground drops abruptly
from the edge of the lawn and looking over it is almost like
looking over a cliff, with the Weald instead of the sea.

dead: I cannot question them. But I am sure that my interpretation is right.

It was of a piece with all the rest. She wrote, she drew, she played. She must have enjoyed her own artistry for she played her music and kept her drawings. If we saw them

The Bishop of London (Dr. Winnington-Ingram) as Mrs. Partington trying to keep the tide back with a broom.

lying about—which rarely happened—she liked our delight in them, but would never allow them to be shown to anyone else. I often begged to be authorized to offer them to some newspaper, for they were generally topical and exceedingly witty. They were, too, in the British tradition of good humour. Their subjects could not have felt anything but amused at the caricatures of themselves, but Effie was immovable. She had a special affection for the Bishop of London * and would not risk even the barest chance of hurting his feelings, though she was more skilful in drawing him than any other. With Hudson she was rarely successful and, though she tried again and again, she never satisfied herself with me. As she could not help sometimes betraying the fact that she was drawing me, I begged to be allowed to see what she had done. Occasionally she let me have one look before she tore the paper in half and burnt it, but mostly I was not allowed even that.

As I said, we might not hear Effie play. When I first knew her she would, very rarely, play for Hudson and me, but even this did not last. Effie played when we were out and we used to steal back to hear: but the moment she knew of it she stopped.

Effie's great and many talents demanded expression. There was the end. I never knew one more variously gifted nor so silent in all her gifts.

It is hard for those to whom Effie is known only by my account of her to believe that with all this she was infinitely attractive. Those who knew her in life and loved her will perhaps feel impatient with me for my fumbling attempts to show her as she really was. When she was well and in the company of those few with whom she felt at ease, she was enchanting. Some of my loveliest memories are of drives with her in the country round South Luffenham. She had a great love of animals, rode with Hudson in the days before I knew them, and was a fearless rider. She gave it up as demanding too much energy, but she always liked a pony-cart better than a motor-car—as indeed Hudson did also. She had a liking—inexplicable to me—for cats and cats for her. I think their detached attitude towards life pleased her and suited well with her shrinking from claims on her which she lacked vitality to bear. She enjoyed their company and was frantic if she missed one long enough to fear that it might

* Dr. A. F. Winnington-Ingram.

have met some mischance. Hudson liked dogs and horses better and would have afforded a horse if he could have afforded anything so costly to keep and care for. I rode with him sometimes on holiday and we enjoyed our rides enormously, yet, as I have said, the memory of my drives in a pony-cart with Effie is as dear and joyful to my mind.

Her gaiety and charm, constantly eclipsed by fear as the moon is eclipsed by a cloud, survived, and even the shock of Bernard's death did not obscure it. I can show her, at least a little, as she showed (or refused to show) herself. Nothing is left of her music, but I, feeling half guilty, give in this book some few of the drawings she left; some paragraphs from her letters, and from the diary which she kept, at highly irregular intervals during the war. It is written in the style of Pepys and, alas! but little was preserved.

She wrote to me after a severe blitz:—

"Do speak to the Man—he will run out to the Air-raid in dressing-gown and bed-socks which look so strange with an Officer's cap."

(About the 1922 General Election):

"Voting was difficult and the voters puzzled beyond words, from the man who didn't wish to vote for Mr. Blank, so 'put a cross opposite *his* name', to Mrs. Barnett who couldn't make up her mind so went to bed on polling day with lumbago."

But it is Effie's Pepysian diary that shows her at her most enchanting. Her best friends—none of whom but myself ever saw it—would be amazed at its wit and gaiety. Here are some extracts. The references are to Dr. Orchard and myself. Dr. Orchard had kindly allowed me to sleep in his house, which was in the Garden Suburb only a few yards from the Shaws', while he and Mrs. Orchard were away on holiday and the Shaws hadn't a spare room. He complained (doubtless unjustly) of theft on my part.* Here is Effie's comment:—

"A most horrid foul day. Myself thrown into the greatest possible twitter by the preacher man from the Conventicle that calleth itself the Free Catholique Church. 'Tis given out he hath Incense and Vestments and cloathes and fal-lals extraordinary for their mighty choiceness tho' God knows I see no likeness to the Archangel Michael in him. . . . He gives it me for certain that that young preacher-woman from the City Temple hath stolen his pillow and bedd-suit (being of French grey, and stripes of rose-pink to make the most gracious effect possible). He be hard put to it to sleep at all and says he will be damned (which is like to be true enough) if he stand it and naught for it I think but the saucy wench must be presst by law, come what may of it. So away, in a measure comforted, but hard put to it to know how to comport myself in this damnable concern. But Lord! the brazenness of the wench she shewing no signs of a fitting shame or repentance and what with the young wenches that do swarm about her for consolation and the old men who do look upon her as a daughter and the losing of her purses and her written discourses (which the Lord knows are not of much value) and her borrowings, supposing her sweet smiles sufficient payment, and her wearing of men's cloathes and neither Leagues of Honour nor aught else shall stop her, it doth all so vex me as never I believe was I so vext before. But it seems the men are now all gone to the warr and we that are left like soon to have naught but women for all work that can be done; a very evil prospect God help us all."

The matter of my thieving did not rest here. I soon had another letter:—

* Since a reader has anxiously enquired whether Dr. Orchard really thought I had stolen his towel, let me here state that he did not!

"HONOURED MADAME,

Peradventure you will wonder at the forwardness of my again addressing you, but I do pray you lay it to naught else but my humble desire to acquaint you once more of certain matters concerning that poor wretch of a preacher man. He to sit again on our door steppe his nose blue with the raw ayrs, and asking our prayers for his pitiful case. This vexes me mightily for I cannot have my family's name brought into publique scandal—also we fear to come in at the door or to come out which doth make the Man madd to be so catcht. It seems the preacher now hath no *bath-towel*, which makes him feel—he says—very sick at heart. This, God knows, is no default of mine but of that Prating Woman who rides 74 miles on the Sabbath day and thieves all the time from her neighbours. Pray God he pay not herefor in an onset of sciatique or be laid up with a vile sneazy rheum by reason of not towelling himself and the greatest shame brought upon me and his Conventicle only by God's grace prevented. So for the easing of his mind I to recommend a sermon at his Free Catholique Church on the text 'Whosoever hath not, from him shall be taken even that which he seemeth to have'. To which the wretch answered me not to be a fool. But the poor wretch weeping so, I confess it moves me to pity, so I did resolve to write to you thereon. Therefore, honor'd Madame, I do humbly entreat you to take what I have here writ with some degree of gravity or seriousness. To this I do faithfully subscribe myself,

Your humblest obedient servant,
E. S."

This strange elusive personality which we knew as "Effie" had the same quality in flesh as in the spirit. I never knew anyone who had the habit of vanishing as she had. One moment she was there. We looked round and she had gone. Sometimes, when I had a headache, she would, if entreated, consent to read to me. The book was chosen, the place found, and I settled down to listen.

After a long silence I would groan impatiently and say, "When are you going to begin"? Silence still. I looked round. Effie had vanished. I could have shaken her. But she was not there to shake.

I confess to finding Hudson's performance just as maddening. In his case the book was chosen by him. He knew much better than I, it seemed, what I should enjoy. He settled himself with pomp, opened the book with pomp and began in a voice that would have filled the Albert Hall. After a few sentences dead silence.

"Hudson, do *go on*. What is the matter?"

"Oh, I don't think this bit would interest you."

Silence again.

Patience is not my strong suit. I soon learnt to deny myself my most cherished luxury—being read to. Unrelieved headaches were better far.

Much and often as Effie and I laughed at the Man, he and she laughed at me no less; which laughter kept our love from *schwärmerei* and ourselves from self-pity.

For under this activity and laughter our love continued and grew. It was, for Effie, peace and security: for Hudson and me, the heart of all we did, the deep centre of our lives. Sometimes we quarrelled, sometimes we wounded each other, but all that never touched the realities of love. I wish we had not hurt each other, but I think, since we knew well that we were both very faulty human beings, we found it not difficult to forgive each other. Hudson had the most perfectly forgiving nature I have ever met. Effie, who found forgiveness hard, even in some cases impossible, was exasperated by him. "The Man doesn't forgive," she used to say to me. "He *never* forgives. He doesn't know what forgiveness means. He simply forgets all about it!"

So he "forgot all about it" when, in the stress of life and

often weariness, I hit out—and hit him. And when he hit me could it matter in the light of his love?

"The hours of pain are all blotted out. Only the joy remains," he wrote.

He wrote that. It was true for both of us. And then:—

"I had such joy and comfort on Thursday. A lovely hour. . . . And we were at the right place, ah! say that you felt it so. . . . You cannot know what you made *me* feel."

We could not always be together:—

"It is your birthday and I have not seen you. Only I have kept it with you hour after hour. I wonder if you have known.

"Yesterday was a hell of depression. . . . Do you know what it is to me, at times like these, not to be with you, not to greet you on the morning of your birthday, not to share your joy? Others may. I may not, though I am nearest to you and I know you want me.

"But I shall see you, shan't I? to-morrow. Surely I won't be too ill again. Five minutes together and we can say more than all the writing in the world can . . . but it is your birthday and I want you to have both *that* and *this*, the poor letter that tries to tell a little and can't tell a thousandth part and yet is *so* dear when presence has vanished. I would rather have a long letter from you than all the treasures that could be given. . . . It is all wonder and incredible—and the loveliest of all is that it is greater to-day than ever."

None of my letters to Hudson survive. He kept masses of them. Then, suddenly, he decided that they must be destroyed. He extracted a promise from me that his should be burnt also, and I kept it as well as I could, but could not lose all. He asked several times if I had destroyed them and I had to confess my fault. There were a few, I said, that must be read yet once again before I burnt them. In the end I failed, knowing that he was certain to go before me and that I should be left alone with empty hands. I hope he has for-given me. He always forgave.

Of my letters he, in the end, kept only the last and destroyed that when the next came. I found my last little note hidden in the leather case containing the "Schweitzer watch", which he kept always by his bedside.

Hudson said his letters to me were "naught" compared with mine to him. As I cannot agree, it is perhaps well that none survive to disprove him. I cannot but think it well that a few of his escaped destruction, for without them how could I make anyone understand what our love was?

"I seem never quite to have touched the utmost heights of happiness save during those weeks by the sea. . . . Even the terrible hours of pain are all *blotted out*, only the joy, the intense joy remains with me. Will it ever be like that again, I wonder?"

I don't know when this letter was written for his rarely bore any date but "Tuesday" or "Your birthday". But I know that if it was never "like that again" after some unfor-gettable experience, it was only because it was lovelier still. We had entrancing days in boats on the Isis or the Cherwell, or bathing in the sea, or driving in my little car in woods. They were more precious than the greater experiences of our public lives. But were they greater? No, I do not think so. Nor did he. To us our love for each other was our one achievement of glory.

At one time we were interested in a book that recalled our own experience—*The Love Letters of Ernst Haeckel*. Haeckel was unhappily married, and when nearly sixty years old he met and loved a woman much younger than himself—aged about thirty. They kept their own austere ideal of conduct, and their long correspondence, with a few days of meeting, was all they had. It is a wonderful story and Hudson and I naturally read it with deep interest and sympathy. I have his copy of the book now, deeply underlined and scored with his famous blue pencil. For a while he was absorbed in it.

He even had the idea that when we could not express in writing all we meant to each other, we should write "see page 158" or some other page, and the words underlined would convey our meaning. It seemed a fine idea, but was never realized since we had only one copy of the book between us, and in any case it never seemed to say exactly what we meant (what book could?). But I cannot repress a chuckle when I find a heavy double underlining of these words:—

"Dear Ernst, you must accustom yourself to the fact that in me you have not found a woman who will agree enthusiastically with everything you say."

It is not with laughter, however, but with very different feeling that I read other marked passages. Here are some:—

"You know that every piece of bread you eat interests me."

"After all, you are my spiritual creator."

(We) "were led and driven by a will outside our own, but we will thank God that a beautiful new world—that you thought lost, that I had never yet seen—has revealed itself to us."

"Must I go on loving you more and more? Those two days were harmony so pure, so perfect—almost as though in eternity! You are right: why may we taste our happiness only drop by drop? But perhaps it is so beautiful just for that reason. And consider, what our twenty-three days have given us in happiness and bliss, other people don't feel in twenty-three years of their stale marriages. *It doesn't matter what one experiences but how.*"
(The last sentence doubly underlined by Hudson.)

Yet the book did not really fit us and Hudson's great idea of corresponding by means of it came to nothing. In spite of many beautiful things, I was repelled by the conviction of these two that they were something quite extraordinary in the way of souls. Both refer to themselves with distressing frequency as "two rare and highly gifted souls". They were so—perhaps: but should they have been so conscious of it? Is not love the same for us all, shaped though it must be by circumstance? There are differences indeed between the love of lovers, of sons and mothers, sisters and brother, friends and disciples. Utterly different they seem sometimes; but love is always life and love costs and love is human and divine—for us all.

It does not take a great scientist like Haeckel or an aristocrat like the unknown Francyska who loved him to make a great love. It takes two human beings who are able to give and willing to suffer. Hudson never thought of himself as a "rare and gifted soul": he only claimed for himself, as I for myself, that our lives had been worth living because of our love.

How often have I been reminded, when with him, of those most true words of Studdert Kennedy's, *"When we are with someone who loves us and whom we love, we no longer ask why we were born or what life is for. We know it is for this."*

Sometimes we tried to imagine what our lives would have been if we had never met or never loved; or, living, parted as once we tried to do. We never could imagine it. We could as well imagine how we could have lived if we had not lived. At the heart of all we were and did was this passion. No blows of fortune, failures, or disappointments could touch that and we could suffer no mortal wound nor be tired of living.

Now that I grow tired and old, and he is gone, I marvel at the immense energy and zest that filled us for so many years. In the post-war stage we were more fortunate than ever in working together. We devoted ourselves to the cause of world peace, believed in the League of Nations, and were sure it could only succeed if it accepted the ideals if not the name of Christianity. Hudson's diary of engagements, and my own, again astonish me. He was not a young man nor I by now quite a young woman, but our years troubled us not at all.

Here are some more of his letters, speaking both of the strain under which we lived and its thousandfold compensations.

"Not well? I knew you would not, could not be. . . . I am so sorry, but it is part of the price. If it is any comfort I am paying too, in utter depression in some hours, just tired-out nerves. . . . So much harder for you these days, because Effie and I can talk all things over and over again and enthuse together. . . ."

"But I had such joy and comfort on Thursday! A lovely hour! Oh never in all the thousands you have given me has there been one more perfect. I can't begin to tell you what it was to me. All the thousands have been exquisite, memorable, but somehow this stands out. Was it the sudden change from misery and missing to *that*? It was not altogether or chiefly that. It was *You*. . . .

"I went away a different creature, not even sad that it was only one brief hour. You brought into it everything that I longed for and it is with me still. . . .

"And we were in the *right* place, ah! say that you felt it so. What you gave me was ours though I had not dared to dream of the lovely, lovely gift. And that one hour was by itself happiness enough for a lifetime . . . ."

"Your birthday! Let us keep it together somewhere."

"Tell me, how is it that now I can feel your abiding presence so much more easily and readily than I did?"

Perhaps it was that I too had learned how to write. I often wrote a little letter to hand to him when we parted. He writes:—

"I had *such* a struggle *not* to read it at once, in the booking-office, almost while your car was still audible.

But I *did* wait until I had a quiet corner to myself. I read it again before dinner, during dinner, after dinner, and I don't know how many times before I reached Paddington. Again when I got there . . ."

"Does anyone know you better than I? Is it possible for anyone to have come closer? Have I not seen you tested and tried by fire for all these years?"

"I have told you *nothing* after all. Perhaps it can't be told, only felt."

It can't be told—at least I can't tell it.

He wished something to be told but not all. It can't be. But Hudson's joy and pride in my work was joy and pride to me also—as mine in his. I told him in very strict secrecy of the Companionate of Honour to be conferred to me. He wrote:—

"C.H.! C.H.! C.H.! Congratulations forsooth? I have no words. There are no words. But I feel like singing a sort of *Nunc Dimittis*! Only I don't want to be dismissed —yet—now. Nothing, nothing, in my life, save *One thing*, will ever have given me one-half the joy.

"Balliol Fellowship. Stanhope Prize, etc., nothing in comparison."

"You tell me so often that you have spoken *badly*. And I laugh. You could not if you tried." (Oh, couldn't I? How often I could and did! But he wouldn't admit it.)

When I was in America he heard that I had spoken of him as a pupil might of his master, and he wrote:—

"I want you to tell me about that New York reporter. Did he know (or did you tell him?) of our work together?

"You lied like a trooper! I your inspiration? And you said 'Yes'! Not a word of truth in it. If ever I have the chance to write about you I will wholly contradict it. It thrilled me to the heart that you should have boldly said it, and I shall never forget.

"But the solid impregnable truth is that in the usual sense of the words neither I nor any human being on earth has inspired you. You have been your own teacher. Your teaching, right or wrong, is your own, perfectly original, derivable from nobody, least of all from me. *I have only loved you.*"

Hudson liked my sermons, my speaking, my books. Except when my work took me away too far, he had no wish to limit me, no jealousy of me.

Often he said what here he wrote:—

"One thing I don't believe you *wholly* know or guess, the *intensity* of my pride in the work you are doing. . . . If only you will not overstrain, work too hard, and kill yourself with hard work—-Oh, don't!"

"Why", he wrote indignantly, "did those dreary fools at Oxford not find you out or understand the capacity that was in you? The very day you were given your opportunity you rose to it and have never stopped since."

Let me hurry to explain that "those dreary fools at Oxford", my tutor and coaches, were far from dreary and still farther from fools. On the contrary, they did all they could to push me into a First Class in Modern History and were defeated by my own complete idleness and absorbed interest in everything but my work. I was sorry at the time that they didn't succeed, but have often hugged myself since for Hudson too missed his First by some inexplicable fluke —inexplicable because beyond the shadow of a doubt he had a first-class brain. He had above all the genius of the teacher. How I loved all those who praised him, all those who spoke of the inspiration he was to them, every one of those keen, fine students whose marvellous teacher he was for so many years. Best of all, for me, was the work he did so often for *my* people, the people of the Guildhouse—who loved him. It was he who, when we were considering how to raise a necessary sum of money, suddenly rose at a Council meeting and proposed that everyone should give, collect, earn, borrow *or* steal £1 and give it me on my fiftieth birthday. There were over a thousand of us, said he, so we should have over a thousand pounds "without any trouble at all".

I was left gasping. I never had a rich congregation and didn't want one, but how we were going to raise £1,000 I couldn't guess. Hudson guessed, and guessed right, for long before my birthday the thousand pound mark was reached and passed. My gratitude was deep and lasting, but so also was my appreciation of that dynamic energy which fired us with a common aim and made us really believe that we could raise any sum we wanted "without any trouble at all".

Time passed. Between our first meeting and Hudson's death was forty-three years. And all that time we loved each other and all that time we loved each other more and more. I do not pretend that we were never for a moment alienated, and I see, looking back, that this was the fault of both of us but more mine than his. The jars that sometimes hurt us arose not from any difference about our relationship but from a divergence in our way of handling it. It was my plan to throw myself into other interests and even other human relationships with energy. I was fortunate in that this didn't really demand a plan: the people I loved and the work I did were so dear to me that in any case, and even had Hudson and I been married, they would have been very near to my heart. And it seemed to me that to give all I could to them was, besides being natural to me, both right and wise for us two. I own that I sometimes gave Hudson grounds for feeling that I gave to others what he felt belonged to him. I thought he should have understood and agreed. He didn't —at least not always. I realized that, partly at the time, but after our marriage more clearly, as I shall show.

Hudson, of course, did the same in many ways and most of the time; but it was his inclination, when we were together, to dwell much on what might have been. He did this without rebellion or resentment but he did it, and I often found the strain unbearable. I wanted to put such thoughts, however dear, out of mind and to concentrate our minds (for it is dangerous to leave them unconcentrated) on our work. For many years we had a standing engagement to read theology together on Saturday mornings, in his study at St. Botolph's Clergy-house. I was not trained to be a preacher and I really needed his help, his teaching, and his books. But it often happened that we were pursuing rather different lines of thought and the reading we wanted was naturally different also. I was always more than content to be in the same room with Hudson, he with his work, I with mine: but in certain moods this exasperated him. Why are we wasting our time? he would ask. What is the sense of our sitting in the same room in silence? Well, we both had work to do and we *needed* to work; but this did not content him.

I thought I was right then not to dwell overmuch on other things. To do so, I thought, made life needlessly hard for us. Now I wonder if I was mistaken—if it was a desire to escape pain—a piece of cowardice of which Hudson would not be guilty. One must not try to escape the pain of life. What do we suffer for if we lose the knowledge it gives by trying to evade it?

I shall never know. I chronicle what we did. And sometimes this difference in our way of meeting life made a rift between us and he was jealous and I gave him cause. I was impatient when he thought I was doing too much. It irked me when he complained that I had other friends more dear to me than his to him. Perhaps he had cause—how can I judge? Was I ungenerous? Was he exacting? I do not know. Only I know that his faithfulness was something that one might dream of but hardly hope to know, and that it continued with utter steadfastness till he died.

"I will be satisfied" (he wrote) "if 1927 is as lovely to us as 1926 has been, won't you? . . . I was just slowly dying when you came, in 1901. I can remember it all exactly. I can remember just wanting to die. Outward things were well with me. I had succeeded with University Extension. I had been made Fellow of Balliol. But I didn't care any longer about *anything*. I had lost, never had, the crowning gladness of life, which is life itself. Without it, nothing is.

"And You came. And you did truly save me utterly."

And another year:—

"It has grown, grown this last year so. But how could it, when it was boundless years ago? Oh! I don't know, but I do love you more, and I believe that every year I shall love you still more. I thought this morning. . . . All these years, in *every* trouble, every anxiety, she . . . has stood by you, helped, made herself part of you, felt not *for* you but *with* you, blessed you, fulfilled you, taken away the smart of every pain.

"You have been all this more than twenty-one years— for more than twenty-five, and nothing has changed, except—every year dearer, sweeter, closer."

"Do I care more? Yes, yes, a hundred times, a billion billion times more (to speak astronomically)."

I wish I knew, I wish I could remember, with what words I answered such letters, but, though I have no record, I know that I contented him.

CHAPTER VI

THE TIME came at last when Hudson had to give up his work. He was growing old and the terrific energy with which he had poured himself out when young and in middle life was now telling on him. He was subject, as ever, to devastating periods of depression, but now he could not fight against them. More and more frequently he was absent from London. All his life he had dreamed of possessing a cottage somewhere in the country to which he could go for a rest sometimes, and for his old age when it came.

There are perhaps few people who realize the dreams they dream for their old age. By a blessed miracle, Hudson did. He found a cottage, not too far from London, which fulfilled them all. It is near Sevenoaks, on a hill overlooking the Weald of Kent. It is fourteenth century and almost wholly unspoiled. It is, in fact, almost incredible. Hudson's constant cry was—"What have we done to deserve this?"—and the answer could only be "Nothing!" Who could deserve it?

Once, when he had had an impacted wisdom-tooth removed and was in great pain, he was given morphia and, as in most such cases I believe, he had a lovely dream.

"I dreamt I was in heaven," he told me.

"What was it like?" I asked.

He was silent for a moment and then said, "It was like this little wood, when the bluebells are out; only without the pain of their passing."

To this little paradise on earth we often came, sometimes for the day, sometimes for longer. Hudson's holidays were spent here always, though I used to wander sometimes with those other friends to whom he a little grudged me. And when the time came for him to give up his work it was here that he and Effie came to rest.

By another miracle—all this seemed miraculous to us—the house next door to the Old Cottage fell vacant a few years after Hudson's settling there and I was able to take it and leave London. Our gardens marched and we could come to each other across them without even going into the lane. At first, he was still doing a good deal of work and I was in full tide. (I am seventeen years younger than he.) But we never regretted the move or thought the distance from London troublesome. Effie, too, was happier, though at first she had the strange recurrences of terror which it was so tragic to watch. They passed more easily now.

It was partly the possession of this almost fairy-tale home that reconciled Hudson to his retirement. Nothing could make it easy, for he loved his people and his work with a passionate attachment. Indeed I feared that, like many men who retire from an absorbing labour, he would die when he gave up work. I under-estimated his still amazing vitality, and he had interests to keep him alive—his garden, his books —and his love. It troubled him that he was older than I and he held on to life so that I "might not have too long to wait". I used to remind him of this when his strength seemed failing, and we counted the people whose deaths were in *The Times* columns, "In his ninetieth year" or more.

But on the whole he was glad at last to give up work. I asked him once or twice whether he missed it very much and he said, "Sometimes"; but he said, too, that he had found the last years of his life at St. Botolph's a terrible strain. A mortal fatigue fell on him. He had had to take longer and longer periods of rest and more and more often to telephone at the last moment to say he could not preach or take his beloved class. The strain of keeping engagements when he was unfit for them, and the failing to keep them when he was quite unable, was a torment. It was, in the end, a relief to make the final break, and instead of dying he renewed his vitality and enjoyed his life in peace and the garden.

To his people the loss was a sore one. They forgave him

all his absences, understanding as few do at what cost he came when he could. Their love and loyalty were lovely. His message to them expresses his love of them:—

Bayley's Hill,
Sevenoaks.
August 6th, 1935.

"None of you can imagine with what feelings of dismay, and utter regretfulness, and almost despair, mingled with deepest thanks and gratitude to you all for your unbroken kindness to me, and my own return of deep affection for every man, woman and child in the Church whom I know —no, it is not possible to look forward to August 13th without a sort of horror and stupid amazement, as though one were going to be hanged, or sent to penal servitude, or something like that.

"There are no words, and we will have no farewells, but this I will write, and I mean what I write. I say then that for the last score of years and more there has not been in the Church of England any Rector or Vicar happier in his work than I, prouder of his folk than I, more grieved to resign his post than I, more ashamed than I that the work has not been done better. . . .

"Let me not forget my manners. My chief object in writing this letter to you is to thank, thank, thank, everybody, all of you who in any capacity have helped our Church to attain to its present position, viz., over 90,000 Religious Attendances every year, and far more than 100 persons every day for private Prayer and rest. I ask one thing. When I am gone, do not forget Dr. Albert Schweitzer, and his glorious work at Lambarene. He needs your help and so few of us give it.

"For the rest, I pray you forgive all faults and offences, sins of omission as well as commission, of my ministry here.

"I loved you greatly, and always shall."

And here are some of the letters he had in return:—

"Words cannot express our feelings when you speak of resigning from St. Botolph's. We have always dreaded the thought of it and always hoped that your health would improve and that you would be spared to us for many years. . . . We first became acquainted with you at one of your Thursday services: since then we have counted ourselves greatly privileged to be able to attend your Thursday Lectures: Mondays, the wonderful new Testament courses in the Little Chapel: Fridays, the Study circle in the Parish room.

". . . Do you remember the first one you held when the bright sunshine was as warm as summer and we all stood in the Church garden and sang our hymns and shewed forth to the world the joy of what Good Friday meant joy in that God so loved mankind? Yet another picture: the children's day at May Queen Festival, the beauty of the scene I have always felt I wanted some great artist to paint that picture for all time, as the Queen kneels to receive her blessing before going out into the garden to be crowned and to watch the revels. Thank you, dear Rector, for giving us such a storehouse of wonderful memories. Ever you will live in the hearts of those who love you."

"You seem to be able to help everybody—you have helped me so much and so often till now the very sound of your voice helps me, and I am sure it is the same with a great many people. Doesn't it make you feel happy to know how terribly you will be missed? . . ."

"My sister and I both treasure your great friendship and as you tell us in your letter in our Magazine you love us all greatly so we in return surround you with our love. 'Love groweth everywhere like a weed.' Truly it has been so in St. Botolph's, far reaching indeed its influence and we feel honoured that we have been privileged to be one of the circle."

". . . Please, please write to Mr. Lambert if you cannot come. He always reads your letters at class and we all then remember you and thank God for you."

"I feel I would like now to thank you for all the wonderful things you have taught me, on Mondays, Thursdays, and Fridays. I will try to be worthy of the great trust of passing on to others the knowledge that is now mine, and helping to bring God's Kingdom here on earth."

Michael Sadler wrote:—

"I have only just heard that on doctor's advice you have been compelled to resign St. Botolph's. I am deeply grieved that your health is not strong enough to support the strain of the great Church where you are doing a work which all who have come under your influence will bless you for, throughout their lives. And what you have done by counsel, inspiration, and warning, by words from the pulpit and in confidential talk and by your writing, will be like radium, animating for years and years the individuals and the Institutions which have come within the range of your compassion."

And a little later:—

"Your letter of Wednesday has just come. No one but you could have written it. The fire of your friendship is unslaked. I never forget you. You are part of my life."

Hudson's activity—his whole personality—was "like radium". The fire of his friendship was always unslaked.

I have so many letters testifying to this dynamic quality in my husband that I cannot choose among them. Many more came to us on our marriage and still more when he died. Here I record only the extraordinary impression that he created and which those who once felt it never forgot.

"He was a great figure in the City," said a City newspaper, "a man who exerted considerable influence on City affairs and in City lives. We may well be proud that we were served by such a man and that his name is inscribed —with those of many other illustrious Rectors—on the gallery of the Church."

Henceforth Hudson was to lead a quieter life. He was strong enough to enjoy his cottage, his garden, and a life without the unceasing toil that he had known since he was a schoolboy, teaching boys bigger than himself by day and teaching himself by night. Few could have endured so long such inhuman toil. Now it took its toll. Though he enjoyed life so much, I was often aware of the mortal fatigue that fell on him at times and left him open to dark depression when it seemed to him that he had achieved nothing.

Only and always the one thing he excepted was our love. He felt, and I did, that it was beyond the reach of time and that it would only grow deeper and stronger as we aged. He wrote of this in letter after letter—"After twenty-two years" and "After thirty-four years", and so on.

"You know, don't you, that although I thought after thirty-four years of opportunity—I knew you through and through, *all* the you, I was wrong. There are things in you that I had not suspected and they have achieved the *impossible*, namely, compelled me to love you . . . as I had never yet done." This was true for me too. The faithfulness of such love was wonderful, but to feel that it increased in passion after so many years and as we both grew old, was more wonderful still. Sometimes this used to comfort us. "If we had been married all these years," Hudson said, "do you think I should still tremble when you come into the room?"

Yet we did not really doubt this for, like all who know a great love, we were convinced of its immortality.

How blessed were we! We had not twenty-three days, as Haeckel and his Francyska had, but many, many days of "happiness and bliss". At first they were mostly days up the river at Oxford, when Hudson used to row all day, his style resembling that recommended by the friends of Mr. Verdant Green—"put your oars in deep and bring them out with a jerk". The boat shook under his energetic jerks and made me crossly, but quite vainly, demand a punt. I believed (and still believe) that this was because he was no punter, and I was more docile than usual because I didn't want him to fall into the river. In any case I could not have persuaded him that I seriously preferred a punt. We went in a rowing-boat.

Later we went to the sea, and in it, but not on it, in spite of Hudson's rowing style being well suited to sea-going boats. We were both bad at being on the sea and this was fortunate as, on this point, had we differed, the case of the irresistible force meeting the immovable obstacle would have occurred. As for bathing we both loved it.

Our long days in the country were perhaps the best of all. I acquired a car shortly after the end of the first World War and both Hudson and Effie took to it after a while. Effie never liked the open car but, when I succumbed to the years and bought a closed one, she liked it better. When she tired of it, Hudson and I still went out for long lovely days, our luncheon in a basket at the back of the car, our tea at a farm or inn.

Hudson was *fun* to go about with. He bought the most extravagant food and tipped everyone enormously. Tipping people enormously was his favourite sport. I can't think how it was that one who had been so very, very poor could become so immoderately generous. Perhaps just because he had been poor? Or perhaps—and more likely—it was his nature. He was a natural giver. Effie was indifferent to money: Hudson delighted in it, as a thing to be given or spent.

I never realized how, in spite of this, he worried about her future. He was never rich and at first told me that he "banked on outliving her". Later, when it seemed much more likely that she would outlive him, he, who simply *could* not save, was hag-ridden by his anxiety for her. It is one of the griefs that haunt me when too late that I never knew how anxious he was. I used to remonstrate with him about his extravagance. Of course, Effie would have been my care if he had died first and, even in scolding him, I told him this and he knew it was so—for how could I ever do enough for her?—but this only increased his trouble, for he hated the thought of adding to my difficulties.

I wish I had not been so angry with him. I ought to have known that he did try to curb his overflowing generosity (though with complete lack of success) and above all I should have guessed at the intense anxiety which, paradoxically, accompanied it. In any case he couldn't have left Effie enough to live on, whatever he had done. I should have tried harder to reassure him. When, after his death, I found hundreds of pages in (exceedingly expensive) note-books, covered with figures, criss-crossed with calculations, showing the retrenchments he planned that he might secure her future, it made my heart ache. Effie never cared about her own future. She knew well that either Hudson or I or both would always be there. Or, if not, she would not have cared to live. But it is hard to know that, owing to my exasperation, Hudson rarely let me know how troubled he was, and to think that I might more understandingly have shared his anxiety.

After all, his *giving-ness* was a delight to me. How could one help loving him for it, even when one couldn't help

laughing at him or raging at him too? I can even remember
with a smile a most characteristic incident—Hudson himself
on his death-bed. He had been worrying the nurse about
something that she could not understand—something that he
wanted and couldn't explain. When I came in she told me
and asked if I could guess what it was. I thought I could, and
going to him I said, "Don't worry about anything. There is
nothing to worry about. You have paid all your bills. No
one has anything against you."

He was silent for a moment and then said, with a faint, but
unmistakable chuckle :

"It will be the first time!"

Hudson's ideas of a "bat" were always on a large scale.
We would go to the theatre—a matinée because "it would
tire me to go in the evening". After the show it always
seemed to him a pity to go home, so we dined somewhere.
After dinner it was still a pity to go home so we went to
another show. This is my idea of a "bat", too. How we
suited one another! Rarely did we get Effie to go with us.
I remember the last time. It was a cinema—a Charlie Chap-
lin film, I think. At the last Effie held back, but we thought
we knew best and dragged her along. She was in misery all
the time and ill with suppressed terrors afterwards. Hudson
was right—she knew how much she could stand, and theatres
and cinemas were not among her possibilities.

What Effie loved was to have Hudson there, myself, and a
few others.

Her mother, twice widowed, came to live with them
while they were in the Garden Suburb and added greatly to
their happiness. Hudson adored her and she was one of the
very few with whom Effie felt at ease. Indeed, she was an
adorable old lady, sane, strong and sweet and gay. She was
as sociable as Effie was shy and no one could resist her. In
one thing only were they alike and that was their utter
absence of possessiveness. Hudson once said to Effie that he
did not believe there was another woman in the world who

could have been happy in such a relationship as ours: she said, after a moment's thought, "I believe Aunt Ada could." "Aunt Ada" was the name we all gave to Effie's mother, and Effie never called her anything else. Even in this most happy relationship it seemed as though she kept life at arm's length and liked to hold back even from the mother she greatly loved.

She was right in her estimate of Aunt Ada who, discussing our threefold love, said she thought it both wonderful and lovely, understanding how much it had brought to us all. Her death at the age of ninety-two left us the poorer and with nothing but sorrow for her going. That is a great tribute.

Effie's range now included Dame Henrietta Barnet, who had for some years lived next door to her in the Hampstead Garden Suburb; and Mrs. Campbell Gordon, a friend of mine and a colleague of Hudson's in his work at St. Botolph's. She was Effie's very close friend and could even persuade her to go for walks in the country round the Old Cottage—a feat which neither Hudson nor I could emulate. I sometimes got her to go for a drive, but a walk? Never! Except with Edith Campbell Gordon! How grateful we were to her for enriching that withdrawn precarious life she surely knows, but I take delight in testifying here. When Hudson and Effie went to live in the Old Cottage for good, she and sometimes her husband came often to stay, and I believe that if she could have lived there permanently— which was impossible, for she had her own home ties— Effie's mind would not have suffered the eclipse which sometimes still obliged Hudson to have a mental nurse for her. She felt "safe" with Edith Campbell Gordon—even, I think, as safe as with Hudson himself, or very nearly so.

As time went on I was more at home and Hudson began to grudge my being away "except for very important engagements". This is a plan of life that I have always detested. So did he, as far as his own work was concerned, for he never cared whether he was asked to lecture to an "important" (*i.e.*, large) audience or a small one. But he didn't want me to be away and this was how he rationalized it! I, too, had fears for him. For many years now he had suffered from a bad heart. In 1928, when I was in Australia, I had received a most alarming letter telling me that he had been to a specialist and was warned that he must give up his work at the very latest in a year's time and, if he did so, might hope to live another three. Fortunately, I had already had a cable telling me to ignore the letter as Hudson was feeling very well and didn't believe a word the specialist said!

It was impossible not to realize, however, that Hudson's life was not a good one from a medical point of view. Equally impossible to expect him to go slowly or contemplate resignation as long as he had long intervals during which he felt magnificently well. This he did, though, of course, there were intervals, not so long, when he fell into depression and felt unspeakably weary. When at last—seven years after his "death warrant", as he called it, had been signed—he did at last give up. To my astonishment, he was able to enjoy retirement and release from the long struggle to keep at work. He loved his cottage home, he continued to read, he devoured newspapers, and reviews and theological books, interspersed with novels that I thought idiotic. We both delighted in rubbish, but unfortunately not the same kind. Hudson loved "Wild West" stories (lumped by Effie under one title—"Gertie of the Gulping Gulch") and I never tire of detectives. He admitted to me once that he never could remember which Gertie he was reading, and I confessed that I was unable to recall "oo dun it" when reading a murder a second time. This didn't prevent me from undying astonishment and indignation at his horrid trash, nor did he cease from disgust at mine. We reviled each other, while Effie, whose favourite reading was Bernard Shaw, despised us both.

But it was his garden that Hudson really cared for most, and it was the fact that he would plan the future of his flower-bed for the next five or ten years that cheered me when he had, a moment ago, threatened me with his immediate demise if I persisted in leaving home for a few days.

What a miracle it was that we were neighbours! I was increasingly lame and even a very short walk was becoming impossible for me. For years Hudson had loved nothing so much as a drive in my car, but now our drives grew shorter and we could no longer go out for whole days. When war broke out I was given a minute "compassionate allowance" of petrol, but it was available only for shopping in Sevenoaks once a week and church-going, also once a week. I was generally away on Sundays preaching, and in any case Hudson, like many retired parsons of my acquaintance, showed a marked distaste for church-going. I suppose they feel they have had enough of it! So our drives dwindled to a miserable shopping excursion once a week. Hudson missed his drives badly at first but, as the years passed, he ceased to want anything much beyond his adored garden. He was too tired.

There is something heart-rending about the gradual loss of physical strength in one we love, especially one who had been superbly strong. Hudson never cared for games but, in spite of his short stature, he had been a great runner and the winner of many trophies. It was anguish to him to realize that he had no longer strength enough to lift me off my feet or even, at last, to see me across our two small gardens in the evening. He persisted in doing this long after his failing strength made it an anxiety to all of us. We used to devise means of watching him as he went along the rough little path and three or four stone steps, never knowing whether it was better to endure the anxiety ourselves or inflict on him the exasperation of knowing that we were trying to take care of him. At last he accepted his fate and would stand at his door and watch me till I was safely up the steps: but he

minded so much—so much. We both hated it, I for his sake,
he for mine.

Still his mind retained its extraordinary grip and he not
only read, but planned to write. Realizing that almost
nothing of all he had thought and taught had been printed,
he and I used to go over the lectures and sermons he judged
his best and plan a book of them to be published "after the
war". Still more he hoped to write a book on the Gospel
according to St. Luke, and I hoped it, too. Though I recog-
nized many of his lectures as masterpieces of scholarship and
style—Hudson wrote noble English—I doubted whether
their subjects were not too isolated and diverse to make a
book: that his studies of the Gospels, and above all St. Luke,
would have made a great one was and is my unshakable conviction. Almost up to the last we were planning it. Hudson
produced summaries, syllabi, notes, and lists of books, and
together we discussed the shape and scope of the work. I
believed that he would write quickly and easily when once
he had started. Alas! he could not start. He had written too
little and spoken too much to be at ease with a pen in his
hand. The faculty had gone. I don't think there ever came
a moment in which he knew for certain that it was too late,
though sometimes he said it was. For my part I fought
against the conviction. I could not accept the verdict. It
seemed to me an intolerable thing that all that thought, that
fresh vision of new things, that matchless power of impart-
ing knowledge should leave no lasting record behind. I have
even thought of trying to write his book myself, now he is
gone. It is beyond me. Only Hudson could have done it. I
don't know when I realized that the book would not be
written. It was not more than a few months—even weeks—
before his death. I doubt whether he realized it ever.

The war touched him very deeply. Sometimes I hoped
that his increasing deafness saved him from realizing that we
lived in "bomb alley", but of course it didn't. He was a
devourer of newspapers and lost nothing of it, and I remem-

ber how, one evening, when the bombers were roaring over our heads on their way to London, he said, in a voice that was almost a cry—"Will that awful noise *never* stop?"

It is true that when a bomb fell on the laurel hedge that divided our gardens he inspected the hole with satisfaction at first, but later remarked with disgust that the bomb "must have been a very little one". Life with Hudson was always liable to bring laughter and tears together.

Even with the horrors of war, his increasing weariness, and the deafness which made him ask wistfully, "What *shall* I do if I can't hear your voice?" we had lovely days of happiness. There were days when the news was good, days when the sun shone, days when we sat for hours in the garden, basking in its loveliness and planning for the future. Once Hudson said to me, "Would you like to be called light-hearted?" A little surprised, I said I supposed no one could feel light-hearted in a world so agonized. He said, "Ah, but there is a light-heartedness that is noble." This light-heartedness was still sometimes ours.

CHAPTER VII

THEN EFFIE died. In the last years of her life she had been happier than, during my knowledge of her, she had ever been before. No demands were made on her and she had neither to try to do things nor to resist the feeling that others thought she ought to try. And for the years after Hudson's resignation she had him constantly with her. I cannot remember his being away for a single night except once when he, Evelyn Gunter, with whom I shared my home, and I, spent a few days by the sea. Effie gradually ceased (I believe) to be much afraid of life. I never knew whether she ceased to be afraid of death, but at least she no longer seemed to be afraid of anything. Her health failed, however, and she grew gradually more and more rheumatic and was often in pain. We could not persuade her to do anything about it and, if she saw a doctor, she told him nothing. She was a stoic in this as in all things. Sometimes she had a cold, but not often, and when she liked to she would come and sit out with me in the garden, and then she was often as gay and laughing as she had ever been in her life. She even made friends and, when people came to the house, she didn't avoid or fear them. It was lovely to see her. I believe it was because she had Hudson always at home.

But physical pain increased. One evening, she sat huddled up in a chair looking so suffering that I begged her to go to bed. When she consented she seemed hardly able to move. At last we got her to the little twisting staircase and half-way up it, when she stopped and cried out that we were hurting her. We waited and after a while she went on and we got her to bed. The next day there seemed nothing wrong except a cold and her now chronic rheumatism, but she continued so lifeless and looked so ill that we sent for the doctor.

He told us that she had had a slight stroke, and must be kept in bed and very quiet. I found it difficult to believe as, though she was very silent, she had no difficulty in speaking and no sign perceptible to a layman of any kind of paralysis. However, one day, as she was sitting up in bed, with the sun shining into her room, I noticed that one side of her face was very slightly twisted and knew that the doctor was right. She didn't know, and after a few days she seemed to recover and even came downstairs for a little while. But then her cold grew worse and her nurse—we had got a nurse for her by then—decided that, as it was a very cold day, she had better not get up. Effie was a little puzzled and asked me "what was the matter with her?"

Effie had had an intense fear of death. She was thought to be dying when her child was born, and told me several times that she thought it was the most dreadful cruelty imaginable that any human being should twice go through the terrible agony of fear which the approach of death meant. She was thinking, of course, of the fact that every human being must die at last and therefore she herself must face death twice. I made up my mind then that, if it were humanly possible, this agony should not happen to her, and when she asked what was the matter with her I said immediately that she had a bronchial cold (a thing she had had before) and that, as the weather was icy, the doctor thought she had better stay in bed. This seemed to satisfy her completely and she fell into a restful sleep. I think this was the last time she spoke except, a few hours later, to ask "where the Man was". Hudson was ill, too, and in bed, but his room was just opposite hers and I knew he would come. I told Effie he was ill in bed, but not seriously: should I ask him to come? She didn't answer and I think she was already unconscious, but I knew what she would want and went to fetch him. He came and sat by her bed with his arm around her—that arm so muscular once, in whose burly strength she had found such touching childlike comfort all her life—and

I left them so. I think, even in sleep, she knew Hudson was there, holding her. It had always been all she asked of life.

It was late and I went to bed, asking the nurse to call me at once if there was any change or if Effie asked for me, whatever time it was, but she didn't, and only the next morning told me that Effie had gone half an hour before. I feared that she might have been frightened, but it seems she never woke and can never have known that she was dying. I thank God for this, but I grieve that I was not with her. I would love to have held her hand and prayed for her most dear and lovely soul as she went. The nurse had not even fetched Hudson and I had to go and tell him Effie had left us.

He had known how ill she was—really he knew that she was dying: but we had believed for many years that, frail as she was, she would outlive him with his greater age and dangerous heart, and when she went it was a shock that I thought would kill him. He seemed unable to believe it and kept shivering and looking so ghastly that I was in terror for him. I had to arrange everything, of course, and knew that he could not possibly go to her funeral; but when the day came he wouldn't let me go either and looked so stricken that I stayed with him.

Is it foolish to mind these things, I wonder? I don't know. But I went downstairs just for a moment while the coffin was being carried out and I felt a pang of anguish at seeing it. There were some friends there who loved her, but I could not imagine Effie going anywhere without *either* Hudson or me; and now she was setting out alone on that unknown way and we could not help her or save her from fear.

But, as Hudson said to me many years before, "No one who knew Effie could be in serious doubt about her soul!" She didn't need me though I longed to go with her, in the flesh, until her dear body was laid to rest. I went back to Hudson, who was sitting on the edge of his bed, stricken and alone. He could not bear the thought that Effie had gone beyond the reach of his protecting love. Ever since their marriage he had been the shield and defence of her strange, frail, and lovely personality. I sat beside him and he put his arm round me and we were silent.

After a little while he said, quite gaily and with a sort of chuckle, "Wouldn't it be splendid if we could go *now*, *together*, just like this?" I said, "It would be lovely. How I should like that!" He said, "You must be buried with me— in the same grave, with Effie. Be sure to arrange that." I said I would, but I don't know whether it is possible. I don't really mind much, though I should like it.

Later on he said, still thinking he was dying, "You mustn't fret. Promise not to fret." I said I would try not to and that it couldn't be long before I came too. He said, with satisfaction, "No, not long. You won't have to wait long."

In the evening Hudson became very ill. For days he was between life and death. He had very little pain, but he suffered a *malaise* agonizing to see. He couldn't rest and was continually tossing and turning, getting out of bed and only with difficulty being helped back to it. Once he half got up and then fell back on his pillows and cried out, "I can't struggle any longer." I begged him not to struggle. I even longed for him to go. Who could wish him to live at such a cost? I said, "Don't try to stay for me. Don't struggle for my sake." Then he saw that I was crying and told me not to and lay back and rested a little while.

I remember that, afterwards, when he was better, he told me how he had wondered why I wept and how the memory of my tears stayed with him. I said I had cried thinking he was dying. He laughed at that and said, in future if I cried, he would know I was expecting him to die. He said he wasn't going to, but again, "when he did, I must promise not to fret." I couldn't promise. I could only promise to try.

Hudson never had the slightest fear of death, but still he wanted to live and his superb constitution forbade him to die. He began to come back to life. After a while he came downstairs; then into the garden; and then with his usual outburst of energy, he began to weed and water, and plan what should be done next spring and "after the war". He longed, as so many did, to see the end of it, and most of the time believed he would.

It was characteristic of our engrained habit of thinking of life always as lived by three that it didn't occur to either of us at first that there was now nothing to prevent our marriage. After a little while, however, I realized it with a sense of shock. It seemed unbelievable. I thought it *was* unbelievable and hoped Hudson wouldn't think of it. However astonishing his powers of resilience were, he was now an old man and his heart might fail at any time. For years I (and he) had known that whenever we parted it might be for ever. I might come home and find him gone. Then suddenly one day, he said to me, "Do you realize that there is now no legal obstacle to our being married?" I said I had. "When?" "Oh, a day or two ago."

We said no more at the time, but soon he began to press me. We couldn't be married at once, of course, but how soon? He reminded me of that old promise Effie had asked of him many years ago; that if she died first he should, as soon as possible, marry me. I hesitated very much and spoke of it to a few very close friends. Some were opposed to it, others vehemently in favour. It seemed unnecessary to risk hurting anyone's feelings since (we said to one another) nothing could add to our love and nothing change it. Why not go on as we were? What difference could it make? In any case, I could hardly go over to live at the Old Cottage and leave Evelyn Gunter who shared Barnfield Top with me and was much crippled with arthritis.

With this Hudson vehemently agreed and said often that "nothing was to make any difference to Evelyn, whatever happened". Yet we both hesitated. On his part was the dread he had of making me "nurse to an old invalid" and also the fear that people who loved me—my known and unknown friends—might disapprove and perhaps be shocked at our marriage. It was the first consideration that weighed most heavily with him. Hudson had a horror of the miseries of physical illness. He hated my being burdened by his. One day I went into his room and found him in great misery. When he saw me he cried out that his heart was broken "because it is too late—it is too late". I accepted this and thought it true. "It has always been hard," I said, "let it be hard to the end." And for a time he also accepted it.

About this time I wrote to a friend who thought we ought not to marry. Here is part of my letter. It will be seen that when I wrote it I had, as I thought, decided against our marriage.

"You are so kind to me that I want you to know the facts about Hudson.

"His entire life has been a sacrifice to Effie. He has always loved her but never been 'in love' with her. She and her mother were left destitute on her father's death after a long mental illness. Hudson knew that she was not normal mentally, and physically delicate. He also knew that she would not consent to have children. Nevertheless (and he loved children) he married her in order that he might support her and her mother. 'What else could I do?' he said.

"Contraceptives are not fool-proof and they had a child. Effie was almost mad with terror. After he was born she was insane for two years. His doctor urged Hudson to have her certified and put into a Home. He refused even to consider it. He had then to support her, her mother, the child, and pay two mental nurses. He did University Extension lecturing at a preposterously low fee, worked like a slave all the week, and came home to an insane wife and two nurses and to his parish and Sunday work. He had terrible fits of depression, but had to force himself to work through them without respite and without rest. By degrees Effie recovered, but was not and has never been perfectly normal, and several times, even since they came to the Cottage, she has had to have a mental nurse.

"When, many years ago, I went to live with them and help in Hudson's parish, I realized that he was living under a terrific strain. Effie's mental condition added to it to an indescribable extent. He could never really relax.

"We fell in love with each other. As I have told you, Effie knew all about it and told Hudson that, if she died, he was to marry me: and we (he and I) decided that we must *never* allow ourselves to think of this or to dwell on any future that did not include Effie. She was an angel to us, but we are both physically passionate and nothing could make it easy for us. It has been hard.

"If of late years he has sometimes seemed inconsiderate in small matters, I ask you to consider that Effie's growing happiness and serenity, her really happy old age, has been bought at a price: the price has been *his* old age, with periods of intense depression and physical exhaustion.

"Two days after her death, he was sitting with me and he said suddenly—'I regret nothing: I would not change anything I have done.' I knew what he meant and said, 'Neither would I.' But if, later on, he implored me to marry him even now and I refused, fearing it must hurt and perplex those who had always loved and honoured him—try to understand his grief. No—I don't think anyone *can* understand it. I don't understand myself—I can't explain why we so hunger for a day, an hour, in which we might call each other 'husband'—'wife'. It is too deep for explanation. What difference would it make? We could not love each other more, our lives would go on as now. I can only ask you to believe that we do desire it, and I as much as he.

"It is not true that he wants or has ever wanted to monopolize me. He has always done all in his power to help me on. Even as lately as 1940 he *wanted* me to go to America, though he knew the dangers and we both realized that we might not see each other again. I owe not only the love of a lifetime, but my work, my career—everything to him.

"We both owe what we have to Effie's unsurpassed love and understanding and trust: but I believe you will see, too, what she owes him, and why it is unbearable to me to hear him spoken of as anything less than she knew him to be—her protector and most faithful guardian."

There are, on the other hand, some who have charged Effie with selfishness because she asked or allowed so great a sacrifice from Hudson when she married him. We did not think her selfish who knew her best. It is true that she looked on him as a guardian and refuge from life which was so terrifying to her. Perhaps it is even true that this was a large part—too large a part—of her affection. No one will account it to her for unrighteousness who has insight enough to understand her fear.

There are people naturally brave—people who literally do not know what fear is as (we are told) General Gordon did not know it. To such people Effie must remain always incomprehensible.

There are others who know fear in many of its aspects. Most of us are like this. We are afraid of some known danger, such as pain or misfortune or death. Our lot is not so easy as that of the fearless, but we know what it is that we fear and we are not always afraid.

Effie was in another class. She feared life and death and did not know why she feared them. I have quoted her own words—"If I knew what I was afraid of I shouldn't be afraid." Can any of us more ordinary beings plumb the depths of suffering like this? I do not believe it possible. But at least I have seen what it is like. I have seen Effie Shaw sitting silent, with empty hands and haunted eyes, staring at nothing—and afraid.

If there is anyone who, knowing this book, condemns her for seeking the one refuge that was open to her, it was not

Hudson and it is not I. Nor would we, nor would anyone who loved her, wish in the end that she had been denied it. It is true that I sometimes cried out, when things were hard for us, *"Why* did you marry her? Could you not have helped and protected her without that?" But I know the answer—No, he could not. No relation, no cousin, however kind, could have done for her what a husband could. No one indeed could altogether save her from fear, but all that was possible he did. And I, too, in my way, small in comparison with his, did what I could—was what I was—to both.

And it must be realized that from her very nature Effie *could* not understand the sacrifice she was asking of her husband. That was an integral part of her problem. To her, passion was terrifying. That her attitude, especially after the illness that followed her son's birth, inevitably forced upon Hudson at last a completely celibate life was not felt by her to be a tragic sacrifice. How could she, who was not normal in this respect, understand what normal people feel about it? (Indeed, what do we mean by *normal* people?)

Effie's illness was not dangerous to herself or others. It seemed to be nothing more than a settled and insurmountable fear of life. Sometimes she "heard voices", but this was only when she was at the worst, and though they filled her with terror she would not or could not tell us what they said. Sometimes, when she begged us to listen, it actually turned out that there were voices—a distant wireless set or people talking at a distance—sounds we had to strain our ears to hear but which Effie described as "a horrible noise". She evidently had at all times an abnormally acute sense of hearing, but even so there was no reasoning with the agony of fear into which her "voices", real or imagined, threw her. All we knew was that she was afraid: she needed defence. Without Hudson she would have had no life in the real sense at all. That sweet and lovely nature could not have known what happiness was. She would have withered.

Hudson and I, whatever we renounced, had full and happy lives. We lived our lives to the full. We had our work—work that we loved—and were neither crippled nor repressed by the discipline we accepted. No one can have everything in this life. It is one of our stupidities to suppose we can. It is one of the root causes of our greed, our lack of discipline, our instability—our unhappiness.

Looking back on my own life I say with conviction, "I regret little, I would change still less."* In our threefold life each of us gave and each took. And all of us were the richer for the giving. Hudson and I by Effie's giving as well as Effie by ours.

* Browning, *The Ring and the Book*.

CHAPTER VIII

THE TIME BETWEEN

AFTER A while Hudson's health improved. With this we began once more to think of marriage, and soon I found he was thinking of it as a fixed thing. He told his friends when they came to visit him that it was so, and it was partly their generous and lovely reception of this surely rather astonishing news that made me, too, begin to think it possible. While I still hesitated he asked in a burst of indignation "whether I was ashamed of him?" No one who has read this story will wonder that I could not answer other than I did. As he said with great content, "Why should we care what anyone says or thinks?"

It is true that I did care, both for his sake and for our friends: but I couldn't care to the point of refusing the joy that had so amazingly become possible. How right Hudson was and how mistaken I! *All* his friends and relations rejoiced with us, and nearly all of mine. Never can I forget their heavenly kindness. My sisters and brothers telegraphed or wrote. Those of my friends who at first disapproved accepted our decision and were glad for our sakes almost without exception; and some rejoiced with us from the first with a joy that inexpressibly touched and delighted us. Above all I owe a debt of gratitude to my friend Dr. Sybil Pratt. Dr. Pratt (like Dr. Mosely who knew Hudson well) was sure he could get through the ceremony; she believed, too, that it was at least possible that happiness such as ours might well give Hudson a new lease of life, and this naturally gave me encouragement.

But Hudson was not strong enough to go and be interviewed by the Archbishop of Canterbury for a special licence, and I, as I have said, felt it would be an impossible strain on him to have the publicity and crowds that a marriage after the proclaiming of banns would entail.* So we had almost given up hope. At any time Hudson might have a heart attack and he loathed the thought of being ill in public. Then Bishop of the diocese, Dr. Chavasse, came to help us. He told us that everything was quite easy if Hudson could come to our parish church in Weald village. This he certainly could do without difficulty, and so it was arranged.

We were married on October 2nd, 1944, and this little record was printed in the *Guildhouse Bulletin* by Dr. Sybil Pratt.

"Although most of our readers will already know of Dr. Royden's marriage, we feel sure that the many old Guildhouse and Little Company friends of both the bride and the bridegroom will be glad to hear more details than appeared in the newspapers.

"Monday, 2nd October, was a lovely autumn morning in the loveliest part of Kent. Our American and South African readers will be interested to know that the homes of both Dr. Royden and the Rev. G. W. Hudson Shaw and the church itself lie in almost unbroken country in the Weald of Kent. This bit of Southern England has won the rather grim title of Bomb Alley and many of the flying bombs were brought down in the neighbourhood. But no bombs disturbed the peace and quiet of that morning and the war seemed very far away. The sun poured into the little country church, resting on Dr. Royden and Mr. Hudson Shaw, who sat on chairs facing the altar, in the chancel, on the scarlet robes of the Bishop and on the tiny congregation of nine.

"These sat on either side of the chancel, so close to the bride and bridegroom that every word could be heard as

* I may well seem to exaggerate this, but when the notice of our marriage appeared in *The Times* next day we were at once in a state of siege by reporters ringing us up and even coming down from London to try and interview us: and I saw I had been wise.

they plighted their troth to each other in the silence of the almost empty church.

"The Bishop of Rochester, who is an old friend of Dr. Royden's family, had expressed a wish to conduct the service himself. He used the Revised Prayer Book and instead of an address read the XIII chapter of First Corinthians.

"The whole service only lasted a quarter of an hour, but it left a mental picture which will not easily be forgotten.

"Dr. Royden wore a black velvet dress with a gold embroidered girdle and a black hat.

"Mrs. Rooper, one of Dr. Royden's sisters, came over from Speldhurst, and Mrs. Robertson, Mr. Shaw's half-sister, came from London, so both families were represented.

"Helen Newman, Dr. Royden's adopted daughter, travelled all night from Scotland and arrived just in time for the wedding.

"Evelyn Gunter and Daisy Dobson were, of course, there and a few old friends, Ethel and Diana Floyd and Sybil Pratt.

"We are sure that all their friends will join with us in praying that God will give to Mr. and Mrs. Hudson Shaw happiness unshadowed and unending and grant that they may live together 'as those live who find their hearts' desire'."

My heart is filled with gratitude to those who were with us in spirit through all this, and I record it here; especially to my beloved family and Hudson's—to the Bishop and to my adopted daughter Helen, and to my friend Sybil Pratt, whose love and understanding helped so much to make everything possible.

After the marriage was over and the notice in *The Times* duly appeared, there was not, in the avalanche of letters that fell on us both, one that breathed criticism or unkindness.

Why on earth should they, some have asked me. Why? I don't know; but like others I have had enough—mostly anonymous—letters of abuse in my life to accept them philosophically and even expect them. We did not have one. I am not so optimistic as to suppose that there were no critics, and occasionally the echo of them reached me by indirect channels; but they held their hands and forbore to write. They left us to our "happiness unshadowed" and I am grateful to them. What my gratitude is to those, known and unknown friends, who rejoiced with such understanding sympathy in our joy I cannot express. Hudson had been sure it would be so, but I had not thought there was such kindness in the world. Even people with whom I had crossed swords in public controversy laid controversy aside and wrote to tell me they rejoiced with us. One of the few who were present at our wedding wrote of it:—

"It was the most *holy* and uplifting service I was ever at, and though I had a large lump in my throat most of the time, I was also very, very happy. To see and know you were both so happy at last, was such a cause for deep thankfulness."

And another:—"I still feel in an ecstasy of happiness over your marriage. When I came back to the ordinary work-a-day world, I had the queer feeling that I had been far away from it, from the war and from everything prosaic and dull. I shall never, never till I die and I hope not even then, forget the beauty of that service and I shall always love that little church. There was to my mind such a strong sense of the presence of eternal things—it seemed to me, while I listened to you and Hudson uttering those lovely ancient vows, that nothing could really hurt or trouble love, that death could not really part you and him nor any lovers. . . . I believe you don't mind a bit about being lame compared to this lovely joy you have. Am I right? . . . When I contemplate the faithfulness and patience and long-suffering of you both all through these long years, I have no words. The Bishop could not have chosen anything to read more appropriate than I Cor. XIII."

"Love never faileth; but whether there be prophecies, they shall be done away; whether there be tongues they shall cease; whether there be knowledge, it shall vanish away—but now abideth faith, hope, love and the greatest of these is love."

Others, not present at our marriage, wrote in the same way.

"To think of your marriage is to feel a deep inward satisfaction—it is right. . . . When I heard of Mr. Shaw's illness—I almost caught my breath, supposing you hadn't taken this step—but you have—and this lovely relationship you have both created has been completed—so that for those of us who love you, there is this deep sigh of satisfaction."

"I wondered at first what it might mean, but, as I thought, the joy to you both gradually pervaded my understanding."

"I know just what — meant when she said your marriage gave her 'the sense of something eternal'. I felt that most strongly during the ceremony. I felt somehow as though all of us there had been taken apart for a while and just for that little time were truly in the Kingdom of Heaven. There was a most wonderful atmosphere—I think every soul in the church was thinking loving thoughts—indeed I found myself loving everybody."

"I am so glad that you have a deep joy, which is also a deep beauty down at the very core of your being. I have said before—but I want to say it again—that I think the story of you two is a wonderful story." (It should have been "you three"!)

"My poorly furnished vocabulary is wholly unable to express what I want to put in words so that I despair of achieving anything at all. I am so happy that I am completely carried away. All I can say is, God bless you. May He give you perfect happiness throughout your married life and Peace that passeth understanding."

"So few dreams come true, and this world seems to ask a long perspective, so to think that one meeting is fulfilled is consolation."

One more letter I must quote because it gave me special happiness, coming from an unknown Arab friend:—

"I like to add my congratulation to the innumerable ones that your millions of friends all over the world are writing or whispering to you on the happy day of your wedding.

"All those who believe in justice and righteousness have followed with admiration your staunch defence of these ideals. It has been a great relief and encouragement to find in this world of power politics and money somebody, like you, who still believes in the eternal values of truth, justice, and moral courage.

"As a Moslem, I listened attentively to your preaching, on the wireless, which did not fail to impress me deeply by the sincerity of its words and by the deep conviction behind every one of them.

"I end by wishing you every happiness in your future life."

I made it a rule long ago never to read anonymous letters and had acquired the habit of looking, almost automatically, at the end of those in a strange hand-writing to see if they were signed or not. In the happiness of those days I forgot to do so and shall always be glad of it. I would not willingly have missed the kindness of that letter.

Ours was indeed, in the deepest sense, a "happiness unshadowed", though it was ours under the shadow of death.

Hudson had gone through the ceremony better than I dared to hope, in spite of the emotional strain. We had both wished to be married in church, and this was one reason why we had disliked the idea of an Archbishop's special licence to be married at home. Now our beloved Bishop had made everything easy for us and the ceremony was short. Our dread was, of course, lest Hudson should have a heart attack and be unable to go through with it, and we were both nervous about him when the time came. But the familiar words of the service—which he had pronounced so often in marrying others—and I, too, sometimes, for I had been minister at the marriages of some of my Guildhouse congregation—came to us with benediction. His hand was in mine as the Bishop read the great chapter from the Epistle to the Corinthians and, as sentence followed sentence, I could feel the relaxation of nervous tension and the benediction of their familiar beauty.

We went from the church and to his home rejoicing. He was well—he had had no attack—we were married. It seemed as if those who had prophesied that happiness would give him a new lease of life were right. How happy we were!

Then suddenly that evening, came an attack so exhausting that I thought he could not live. He had gone upstairs and I was out of the room at the moment. I was called and found him—as it seemed—dying. Dying! At that moment! I could not bear it. Once I could tell him, once I had told him, not to struggle—not to fight death for my sake—but now! I cried out to him not to go, not to leave me, and even at that hour my voice reached him. He heard me and he turned and came back from the shadow of death.

With his almost miraculous power of recovery he fought through a few days of exhaustion and began to live again. On the day after our wedding he said to me, "How long have we been married?" I looked at my watch. It was five minutes to twelve. "In five minutes," I said, "we shall have been married exactly twenty-four hours." Again and again he put that question to me half jestingly—"How long have we been married? How long have you been my wife?" Three days—a week—a month—two months.

Two months—two months of joy and grief. In that short time Hudson recovered, gathered strength again and again, got up and dressed, came down into his beloved garden, planned its future, laughed at me when I reported that someone had lived to be over ninety and promised that he would try to do the same.

He said to me in tones of infinite content: "I shall never be jealous again, of your friends or your work or *anything*; for, after all, you did marry me."

I had never fully realized how he sometimes felt about my work and my friends—my friends especially, for he was not in the true sense jealous of my work at all, but proud of it; he only minded its separating us. Even then he never resented this if it were for something he thought worth while. I did know that he was a little jealous of my friends, for he told me so, adding that I should be jealous, too, if he cared as much for his woman friends as I for my men friends—or shouldn't I? After due consideration I had to admit that I should, and this pleased him mightily, for he could not understand a love that had no element of jealousy in it. He even said once of Effie that she couldn't really love him or she would be jealous of our love. This made me angry, for I knew it was the very quality of her love that it had no element of possessiveness in it. And Hudson agreed and said that he did know that so it was.

But again and again came attacks which sapped even his strength and at last forced me to realize that he was losing ground.

It might be thought that this time was one of unmitigated suffering: on the contrary, it was lit up with joy that we had never known. Our longing that we might "even for a day, an hour, call each other husband and wife" was fulfilled.

There are times when joy is so complete that one ceases to ask, "Have we deserved this?" or, "Can it last?" Times when we ask nothing, when there is nothing to ask, when time is timeless. So it was with us. What pain would we not have endured for such a heaven? What does it matter that our time was short? Is infinity short?

One consolation I had which is not given to all: it was that with all his love of life Hudson was never afraid of death. He wanted to live. With all the hated disabilities of increasing weakness he still wanted life. When I counted up the nonagenarians in the columns of *The Times* he laughed at me, but he himself would sometimes say with longing, as the days shortened and winter drew on, "If I could have *one* more spring, *one* more summer!" We told each other that the war would be over and we could go for drives again and see the loveliness of the countryside. It was a beautiful dream. But we knew it might be only a dream and Hudson would speak of death without anxiety or fear, only once more promising me to live as long as he could that I "might not have long to wait". How I pity those whose beloved are fearful and must not be told they are dying! How dreadful to have to be playing a part when time is so short!

I don't know when I knew that Hudson was leaving me. He knew it before I did, I think. The knowledge came near me when he ceased to want to get up and dress. He had always hated staying in bed and disobeyed his doctor's orders when told to do so. Now his doctor urged him to get up and he no longer cared to. He would try, to please me, for I knew how ill a sign this languor was, but gradually he ceased to try. He was too tired. More than once when our eyes met, he gently shook his head. I wanted to say, "What is it? Why do you shake your head?" but my courage failed me. I did not want to hear him say he was leaving me.

Gradually he did leave me. The day came when Hudson's doctor told me he would not live more than twenty-four hours. I sat beside him, counting the moments, but now I didn't try to call him back. He wanted to live, but the struggle was too great. That mortal fatigue which had possessed him often when in the height of his powers was no longer to be denied. I could not wish him to endure it longer.

He fell into unconsciousness and in his sleep he died. He had no pain and I was with him, his hand in mine.

We had had forty-three years of work and love and we had been married eight weeks and three days. For all this I thank God.

CHAPTER IX

Even the sympathy of those who loved us and rejoiced with us on our marriage was not lovelier than that which surrounded me when Hudson died. I record some small part of it here, because it proves to me our strong conviction that the love we felt for one another was not ours only but a part of that love which others also understand, which others feel. In this again Hudson was utterly right. He never claimed that he was a person of unusual moral stature, whatever he thought of me—he was "a good lover" and in this was all his pride. That I, too, was a good lover was his high praise of me.

So others did understand and of their understanding here are records:—

"It was only last night that I got the tragic and overwhelming news of your husband's death . . . and now what—oh what can be said? . . . I don't even know if you got the letter I wrote when I got news of your marriage* —but I do hope you did, for I meant—from the deepest feelings I'm capable of—all the good wishes I tried to express—and now how apparently futile it was! But is it really so? As I get older the sense of life narrowing down to a sort of vanishing or escaping point, is tempered by a sense of some (even if vaguely apprehended) purpose— and a consequent feeling of thankfulness at being allowed so much fruitful work and happiness. And you have surely an abiding—even if temporarily broken—sense that you have given something—and that of deep import—to your generation . . . and no happenings, however tragic, should cancel out the sense of your immense gift to multi-

* This friend was in America, but I had had his letter.

tudes of men and women . . . you who have touched and quickened us, and taught us that love lives by spending itself. God bless you and give you peace."

"The world will look so empty for a time. But I believe the peace which surrounded your Hudson at the last will have made you thankful that the strife is over. . . . I shall always consider it a great privilege to have known that ardent, generous spirit from whom so much love has flowed, to whom so much has been given."

"It seems such a platitude to say it is all for some good purpose—everybody says that kind of thing, and I never think it carries much weight. But still, as the call did come to Mr. Shaw, one feels that he must have been more content to go because you had had the joy of belonging together."

"Love is timeless and abiding: God's love, your love and his love . . . and we *know* that *all* things—even the sorrow, the agony, the desolation, which He knows and shares with us—work together for good to thêm that love."

"But to realize this in the hour of actual darkness is not possible . . . it is later on that, by His Grace, we can look back and begin to realize that the sorrow is the root of deeper joy: that the loss is not *really* loss. People say glibly that 'time heals'—that is not true . . . the sorrow abides but love does somehow transmute it."

"It would have been less hard to bear if only you had had him even for a year. You would have had so many happy memories of the precious days when your love and care made life for him a time rich with happiness and content. Since that could not be, at least you have the knowledge that for the short time you had him for your very very own you were able to give him comfort and peace."

"It must, I am sure, have caused you much thought before you could make up your mind to fall in with his wish (and on his part too) and yet, although I cannot pretend to know much of the circumstances which weighed with you, I am sure you were right. You must have made him very happy, and just at what was to be the end of his life, when happiness is so precious, so longed for and not often won."

"He is in his celestial garden where his bluebells do not pass. And where, no doubt, the lilies bloom freely and do not disappoint him. You gave me his Alderley Prayer Book. . . . I love the markings in it, and the altered words; and the lines crossed out with heavy indignant pen that he did not believe and would not use!"

"You have only had two short months of 'togetherness' —yet into it must have been crowded a lifetime of experience. The fact that the time you had was dimmed by his illness will be offset by the fact that you were able to 'encompass' him during the time. And I can well imagine the sheer joy and solace this must have been to you both."

"These two months were well worth while and will make a vast difference to the rest of your life. . . . He belongs to you still and will do for all eternity. You will find it easier some day to cross the River, knowing that he (with all his powers restored) is wading out to meet you from the other side."

"I am utterly convinced in my heart, that your marriage was a lovely beginning and that you and Hudson will spend many happy birthdays together—in surroundings you both love, with no shadows to darken your gladness."

"You will not grudge him the delight of going on in front of you a little—he will be getting ready the house where you will live together. I don't believe that you will miss one single bit of the happiness you and he have waited for so long."

"My daughter remarked 'how tragic so beautiful a marriage lasted so short a time', and I said 'at least Maude had what not one woman in a million ever gets—a great man who loved her for her husband'.

"You gave all that mattered in his life to your beloved. It seems that what hurts only you—not him—should be bearable."

"We both felt (and said to each other) how glad and proud you must be that you had the courage to do as you did and give him the happiness of these last days."

Dr. Schweitzer wrote:—

"Alas! as a doctor I know what a terrible illness angina is and how little we can do to arrest it. I am so thankful to know that he (Hudson) died without pain. I shall always deeply regret that I did not know him as well as I so much wished because during my visits to England I was always exhausted with work and obsessed with fatigue, and the hours that I could give to myself and my friends were very rare. But that is my life. . . . And the watch which is associated with one of the rare hours which I was able to spend in tranquillity with him is now with you. It gives me great happiness to know that it is in your hands and guarded by you. It is a pledge of friendship between him and me, close friendship which came into being at the moment when we saw each other for the first time! Many times I think (in the midst of my work) of you and your sorrow, dear friend. My wife and I send you heart-felt sympathy."

CHAPTER X

LOOKING BACK

HAVE I, I ask myself before closing this record, written truly in writing so little of the discords and the wounds Hudson and I suffered at each other's hands? In the past I have sometimes smiled at the way in which people speak of their dead, as though they had no faults and no unkindness. "He never gave me a harsh word," they say, or "We never had a moment's difference." And I who knew them knew it was not true. Of Hudson and myself then, I confess that we had quarrels and differences that went very deep sometimes. We sometimes parted in anger, we sometimes said cruel things. I do not plead in extenuation that our lives were hard, for most lives are hard, and some do better and bear hardness better than we did. But I understand now why people speak of those they love who have died, in a way that seems to the onlooker insincere. We are not insincere, only we truly find it an intellectual *effort* to remember anything in them that was not lovely. The wounds remain only in our own unloveliness. I bear in my heart the scars of the wounds I inflicted on him. I hope he bears none. As Effie said— "Hudson never forgives anyone—he just forgets all about it." I, too, most easily forget the hurts I suffered and some day I shall even forget that I hurt him and live in that "un-shadowed joy" we knew so often even here.

Among the many letters I received when we married were some whose writers in their kindness supposed that my motive was that I might take care of him. I acquiesced. It was indeed a joy to know that I might do that. We had hoped that he might renew his strength (as for a time he did) but, in any case, unless a bomb fell on me, it was humanly certain that I should outlive him and that it would be impossible for him, now that we were married, ever to live a lonely life without the care of one who loved him best of all. This was a joy which many will know and understand. It was, of course, more difficult in wartime to see that Hudson had everything he needed. Nursing and even ordinary care were hard to come by, and but for the love and self-sacrifice of my friends and his* I do not know what I should have done. I remember them with passionate gratitude, because I know they loved my husband as well as myself. With their help it was possible to give him nearly all he wanted, though even now I cannot remember without a pang the things, so small and yet so necessary to the happiness of the old, that he would, as a matter of course, have enjoyed in happier times. At least, I could be with him. How many thousands in this tortured world have had no such consolation!

But I didn't marry him for this. I married Hudson because I loved him. Was that so strange as to need saying? I do not think so, and I know that many knew it too and understood us.

What is, however, incomprehensible to me is not the wonder why we married, but the assumption that we had always been lovers in the accepted sense of that spoiled word. Some—not of those who knew us, but only strangers—thought this must have been so, not with malice but in kindness. And these asked why we didn't go on as before—why did we go through a marriage ceremony?

This did astonish me. I know, of course, that the ceremony means little to some and nothing at all to many. It would be an impertinence to condemn people who act, in spite of convention, as they in their conscience believe to be right. I know such people—everybody does. It is hypocrisy to pretend that a "ceremony" makes good what is not good. But what is difficult for me to understand is how such

---

* I give myself the pleasure of recording the names of those who carried most of the weight—Joan Brazier and her mother, Mrs. Hawkins, Daisy Dobson, and Ethel Floyd.

relationships can be kept secret without loss. To us—Hudson and me—that would have been impossible. We could not have done it. I say *could* not, and mean it literally. I am not a reserved person, and always find it easier to share than to withhold my joys and griefs from the people I love. Hudson would have found it absolutely impossible. He had a certain simplicity which is a quality most lovable and one generally found in those who also have the quality of greatness The really great nearly always have it, though not always. Hudson had it. With his fine intellect and power he was yet childlike in a sense that was never childish, and anything furtive or conspiratorial would have been in him incongruous to the point of absurdity. I have already told how, the moment we had agreed that we *wished* to marry, even though it might be impossible or unwise, Hudson began to tell all who came to the house that it was to be so. One friend after another came hurrying over from the Old Cottage to congratulate me—(How kind they were—Hudson's relations and friends—how adorably kind!)—till I gave up assuring them that perhaps it could not be—that I feared emotional and even physical strain for Hudson, and that it was for the present only a dream. It was no use. Hudson could not keep a secret! Not even the secret of a dream. Rather than attempt such a thing we would have parted. That others, while suffering acutely from the need for secrecy, yet endure it, I know well and only record here that we could not. How strange are our hearts, how many different ways they have of loving!

What seems to me really inexplicable is the assumption that we—Hudson and I—could have had an illicit love and continued with the work that we were doing. We both called ourselves Christians. We were not only committed to a Christian way of life but we took it upon ourselves to teach others. Hudson was a priest and I, though I was refused ordination to the priesthood of the Church of England on account of my sex, preached in the name of Christ. I preached and wrote on sex morals and upheld what I believe to be His teaching. Hudson never, if I remember rightly, preached on this subject, but I know that when he was called on to marry young people he always talked to them beforehand and, in his talk, upheld the standard of chastity before marriage and faithfulness in it. How could we do this if we didn't believe in it? Are ministers of religion so deeply dishonest as to justify the assumption that we did? To what depths of insincerity were we supposed to have sunk?

I know there are priests and ministers who do not accept the Christian standard of sex morals. I know there are honest differences as to what Christ's teaching actually was. But about us two there could be no mistake. We *taught* a certain standard, and whether we were right or wrong no one could doubt that we did teach it. It was surely a dreadful indictment of our honesty to suppose that, in secrecy, we not only did not believe what we taught but actually defied it in our lives. I wish those ministers of religion—and they are not a few— who do not hold the view we did would make it clear that they do not. To my mind it is not enough to be silent about it. If these men think we are mistaken about the teaching of our Lord, is it not their duty to tell us so? There is enough suffering in the world without uncertainty as to whether we are perhaps enduring abstinence, or suffering from a sense of guilt, for no reason.

Hudson and I at least were in no doubt. We knew what we ought to do and, while we only judged ourselves, we advised and taught only what we lived, when people asked our advice.

It is perfectly possible to live by one's own standards, even "resisting unto blood" the desire to live otherwise, without for a moment judging other people. But I ask myself what it was, with Hudson and myself, that made it so possible?

First of all, I put the trust and love that Effie gave us both. Those who have read so far as this will agree. "Tell me one thing," said a friend, "how could you help making her jealous?" The answer is in herself. She was not jealous, she didn't know how to be possessive. There are such people, there is such love. Hudson and I could not have loved like that: if Effie could not we should have parted.

I do not believe that Hudson and I could ever have betrayed her trust. Could anyone?

It was also impossible for us to betray ourselves. Homes and families and traditions go deeper than we realize. Both Hudson and I had, in different ways, been impressed with a certain way of life which made some standards harder to set aside than they would be to men and women who had never known these traditions. This will seem to some a misfortune implying a lack of freedom and spontaneity in our emotional life. I set it down here only because it is a fact, and we did not think of it as bondage but as a standard.

But greatest of all was the love of each of us for the other two. This may seem a contradiction in terms or an admission that our love—Hudson's and mine, that is to say—was lacking in passion, and of a rather inhuman kind. No one who had ever known the impact of Hudson's volcanic personality could think that. I remember the cry of pain in his voice when, one evening, as twilight fell and we were coming back from a ride on Dartmoor, we saw the lights coming out in cottage windows as we passed; and suddenly he said—"Every peasant in the land can have to-night what I must never have." Hudson had rather a strong, even a harsh voice, but, as I have noticed more than once in this book, it had a strange power of moving and shaking the heart when he himself was deeply moved. It shook mine then.

For myself I can only say that he was content with me.

How then did our love make hard things almost easy for us? By our conviction that we were more fortunate in loving as we did than others who loved less.

In a very sympathetic letter, written when our marriage became known, the writer spoke of the pain I must have suffered when I celebrated the marriages of happier lovers. I never did. I always delighted in this privilege. To me, and to Hudson too, I know, it was a lovely and joyful one. Some of those I married will perhaps smile at us, but I think it will be a kindly smile, when I say that the thought of envying others never crossed our minds. How, even with their fulfilled love, could they be as blessed as we were in ours, though unfulfilled?

I write these words with consideration, for I want to be sure they are true. Yes, they are true, and they are the deepest truth about us, even though we suffered. For the real temptation that comes to lovers like us was not that we should betray each other, but a quite different and more subtle one: it was the temptation to self-pity. Against this we did fight. We knew it to be cowardly and poor and we would have none of it, but it did sometimes come upon us unaware, and it was the dread of it that made me afraid to dwell too much on what might have been. How could I think myself the most blessed of women and yet be sorry for myself? Hudson, a simpler and greater soul than I, could speak more easily and naturally of what we fore-went. To me it was a temptation, to him a relief. Either way, we put it behind us.

I know well how many ways there are of loving and how many judgments on those ways. I know how what seems right to one seems error to another. All this is not my concern here. I salute all who love—"all those who travel on love's trodden way". But most of all I salute those who have taken our way, Hudson's and mine, and have not pursued it to the end as we did, because they had no such third as we had—no Effie with her surely unique love for us both. For them the way has been harder still. Yet for them also it must be joy to know that they can say—

"Ich habe gelebt und geliebt,
Geliebt und gelebt".*

---

* I have lived and loved,
I have loved and lived.

During the last few years our love deepened and streng-
thened. Hudson used to say to me sometimes in the early
years, "Can we go on loving like this always?" And I said,
"We shall love better." This was never more true than when
we passed middle age and grew old. There came an added
intensity to our love which increased even during the last
months and weeks. It lost nothing. I could not have believed that love could be so full of passion in one so old as
Hudson. (He was eighty-five when he died.) His vitality
and force might be less in other ways but in love never. He
had been used to say, half jestingly—"When I can hear your
footsteps coming up the steps" (to his garden-room) "without my heart missing a beat I shall know I am really dead."
He never did. I was dearer to him when he died at eighty-
five than ever before. So was he to me. During the short
time before our marriage and after it, to be away from him
was grief, to be beside him all I asked of life.

We three shall meet again. I know it.

> "Hieme et aestate,
>   Et prope et procul,
>   Usque dum vivam,
>   Et ultra."
>
> ("In winter and summer,
>   And near and far-off,
>   As long as I live,
>   and beyond." *)

* Epitaph on a grave in Sicily, found by Hudson and sent by him
to me.